THE COMPLETE ORGAN PLAYER

Book 1
by Kenneth Baker.

This is book one of a brand new edition of 'The Complete Organ Player'.

In this new book one, in response to many requests, I have expanded and developed the text for the benefit of those students teaching themselves. Instructions, relating mainly to fingering or timing, appear in some of the pieces.

As before, audio tapes, including all the songs performed by me, together with additional relevant teaching points, are available from your dealer, or from Music Sales direct.

Four new songs appear in this new book one (more were possible in later books, six being the average), and I have up-dated all 'suggested registrations', putting them on the page to which they refer, rather than on a separate page, as in the earlier edition.

I hope you like the new look.

Yours,

Kenneth Baker

Kenneth Baker.

Wise Publications
London/New York/Sydney/Cologne

Exclusive Distributors:
Music Sales Limited
8/9 Frith Street, London W1V 5TZ.

Music Sales Pty. Limited
120, Rothschild Avenue, Rosebery, NSW 2018, Australia

This book © Copyright 1977 & 1987 by
Wise Publications
ISBN 0.86001.381.2
Order No. AM 19431

Designed by Sands Straker Limited.
Cover illustration by Howard Brown.

Music Sales complete catalogue lists thousands of titles and is free from
your local music book shop, or direct from Music Sales Limited.
Please send £1 in stamps for postage to
Music Sales Limited, 8/9 Frith Street, London W1V 5TZ.

Unauthorised reproduction of any part of this publication by
any means including photocopying is an infringement of copyright.

Printed in Great Britain by
St Edmundsbury Press Limited, Bury St Edmunds, Suffolk.

Contents

About This Book, 3

Layout Of The Keyboards, 4
The Black Keys, 4
Names Of The White Notes, 5
Middle C, 5
The Pedalboard, 6
Keyboard/Pedalboard Guides, 6
Your Position At The Organ, 7
Fingering, 7
First Melody Notes, 8
First Two Chords, 8
Pedals, 9
Chord Practice, 9
Musical Timing, 9
Other Time Notes, 10
New Chord: F6, 14
Ties, 15

Rests, 15
Pick-up Notes, 15
New Melody Note: A, 17
New Melody Notes: B, C, 20
Four-note Chords, 22
New Melody Notes: D, E, F, 23
The Beginnings Of Rhythmic Playing, 28
New Melody Note: G, 28
Quavers (Eighth Notes), 28
Quaver (Eighth) Rest, 28
New Melody Note: High A, 31
New Chords: Am7, D7, 32
Dotted Crotchet (Dotted Quarter Note), 34
New Melody Notes: Low G, A, B, 36
Sharps, Flats, And Naturals, 38
New Chord: C7, 38
Two Pedal Notes Per Bar, 38
New Chord: Dm7, 42

Songs

Barcarolle, 13
Blowin' In The Wind, 24
Eight Days A Week, 27
Every Breath You Take, 32
For He's A Jolly Good Fellow, 18
Goodnight Sweetheart, 42
Gonna Build A Mountain, 31
Jingle Bells, 14
Largo, 11
Lightly Row, 12
Love Me Tender, 23

Merrily We Roll Along, 11
Michael Row The Boat Ashore, 17
My Own True Love, 36
Release Me, 39
Silent Night, 35
Skip To My Lou, 29
Super Trouper, 30
Top Of The World, 40
When The Saints Go Marching In, 16
Where Have All The Flowers Gone?, 26
Wooden Heart, 20

Reference Section

Keyboard/Pedalboard Chart, 44
Dictionary Of Musical Terms, 45
Chord Chart, 48

Layout of the Keyboards

The keyboards of your electronic organ look something like this:

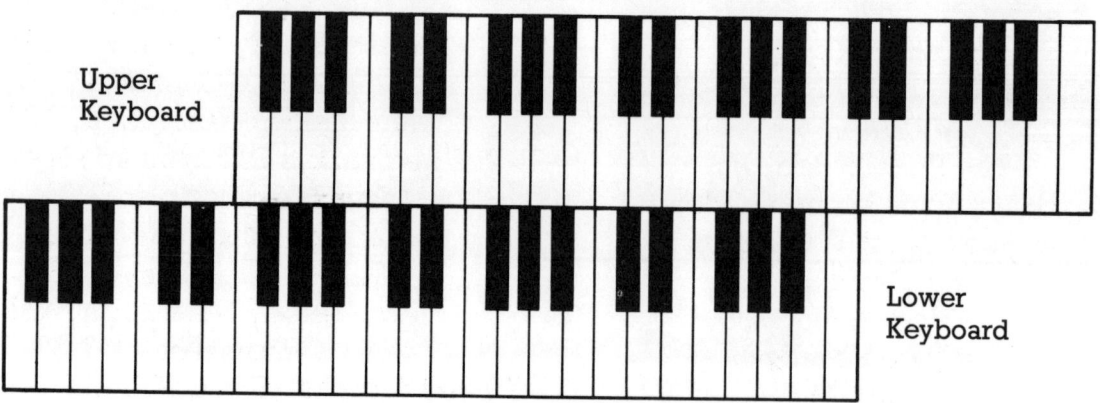

The Black Keys

Your black keys are grouped like this:

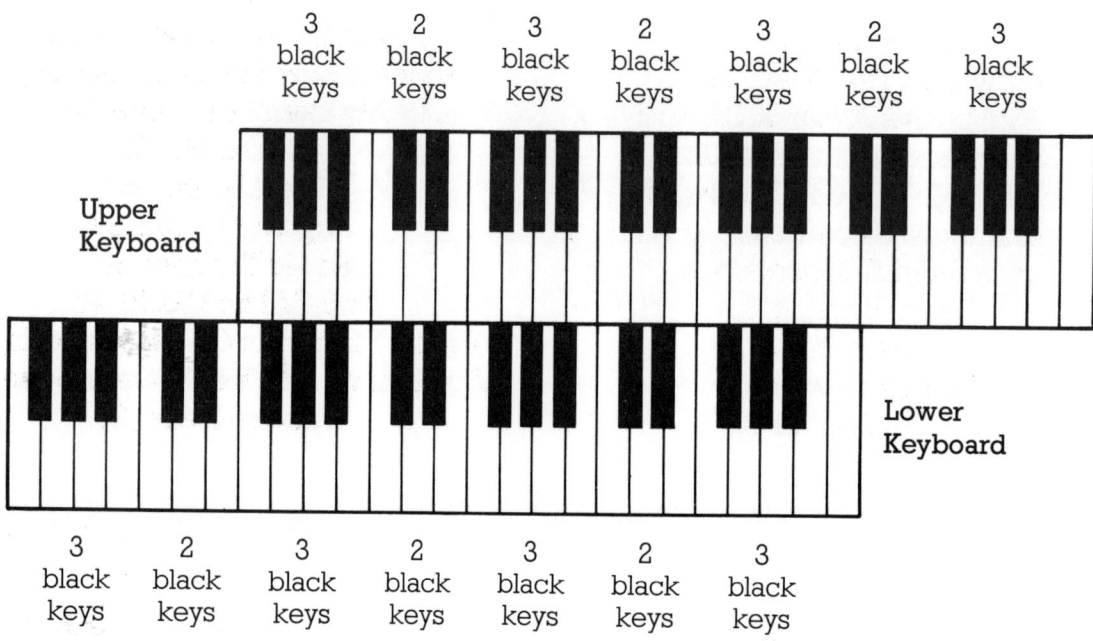

You need these black key groups in order to locate the white notes.

Names of the White Notes

Here are the letter names of the white notes:

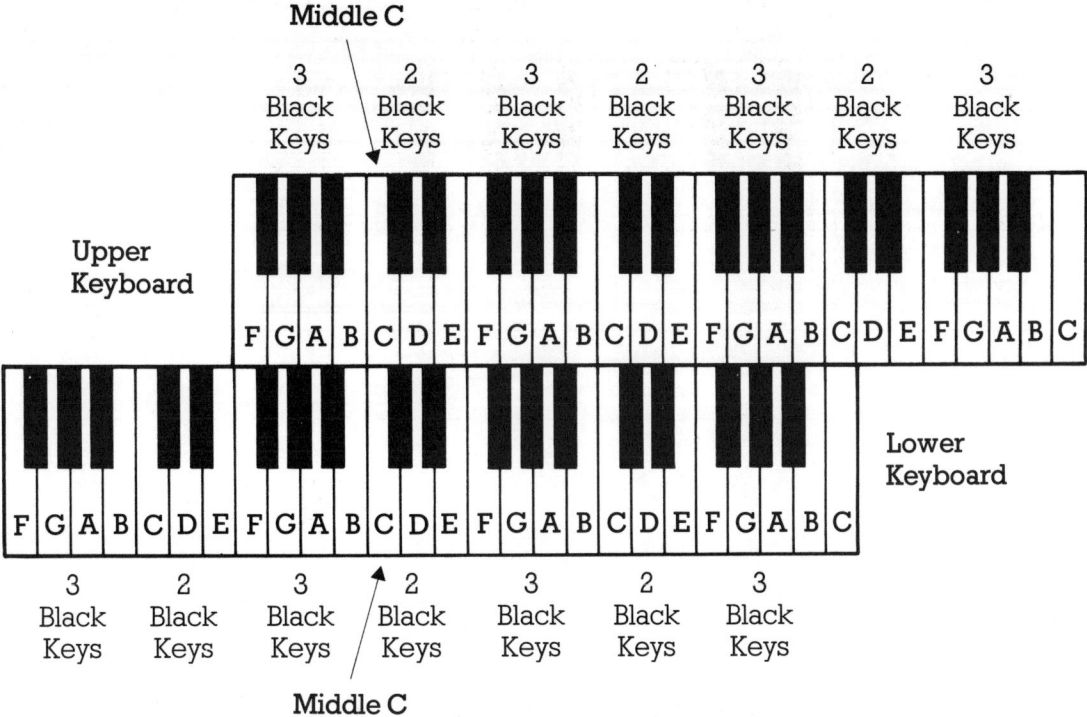

Notice how the notes on the two keyboards line up: the C's on the upper keyboard lie directly above the C's on the lower keyboard; the D's on the upper keyboard lie directly above the D's on the lower keyboard, and so on.

Middle C

C is probably the most used note. You have four or five C's on each keyboard. As you go to the right they get higher in sound.

The C in the middle of the range is called 'Middle C.' You have a Middle C on each keyboard, and they lie one above the other. Refer to the above diagram for the position of your Middle C's.

The Pedal-Board

This is simply a keyboard played by your left toe. It looks something like this:

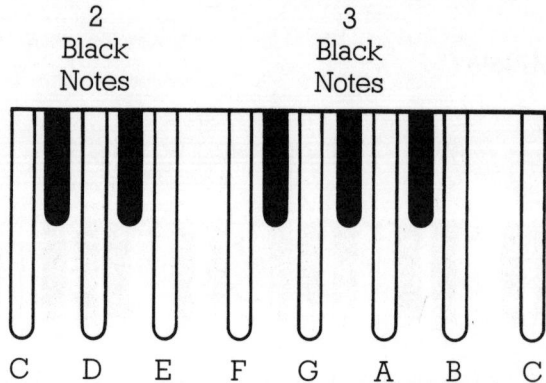

As you see, the notes on the pedalboard follow exactly the same pattern as the notes on the keyboards ('D' lies between a group of 2 black pedals, 'A' lies in a cluster of 3 black pedals, and so on).

Keyboard/Pedalboard Guides

Included in this book are cardboard keyboard and pedalboard 'guides,' which will help you find your way around the notes in the early stages. Don't become too dependent on these guides. Learn the names of the notes as soon as possible, visually, like this:

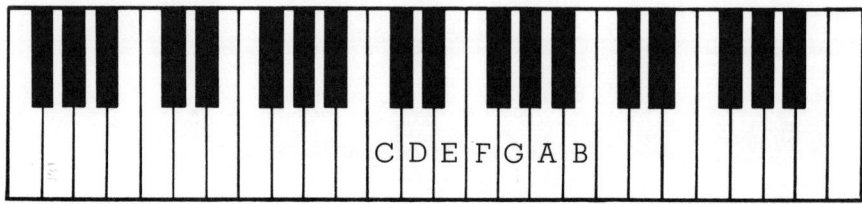

C lies to the left of two black notes. (This applies to every C, including the pedals).

E lies to the right of two black notes. (This applies to every E).

D lies in the middle of two black notes.

F lies to the left of three black notes.

B lies to the right of three black notes.

G lies to the right of F.

A lies to the left of B.

Since there are only SEVEN letter names to learn: C D E F G A B, it shouldn't take you too long.

Your Position at the Organ

Sit (preferably on a proper organ stool of the right height), opposite the Middle C's on your keyboards.

Switch on the organ, and select a 'registration' (a sound set-up). I have given suggested registrations at the beginning of each piece, but feel free to use your own, if you prefer.

Place your right foot on the 'swell' (volume) pedal. Adjust the volume to an easy listening level, then leave your right foot alone.

NEVER PUMP THE SWELL PEDAL INDISCRIMINATELY.

Rest your left foot on the carpet until you wish to play a pedal note. When you do play, use your toe only.

You will normally play the 'melody' with your right hand on the Upper Keyboard. You will normally play 'chords' (groups of notes) with your left hand on the Lower Keyboard. Your left toe will play low single notes, called the 'bass,' on the Pedalboard.

Fingering

The small numbers beside the written notes tell you which fingers to use. Here's how your fingers are numbered:

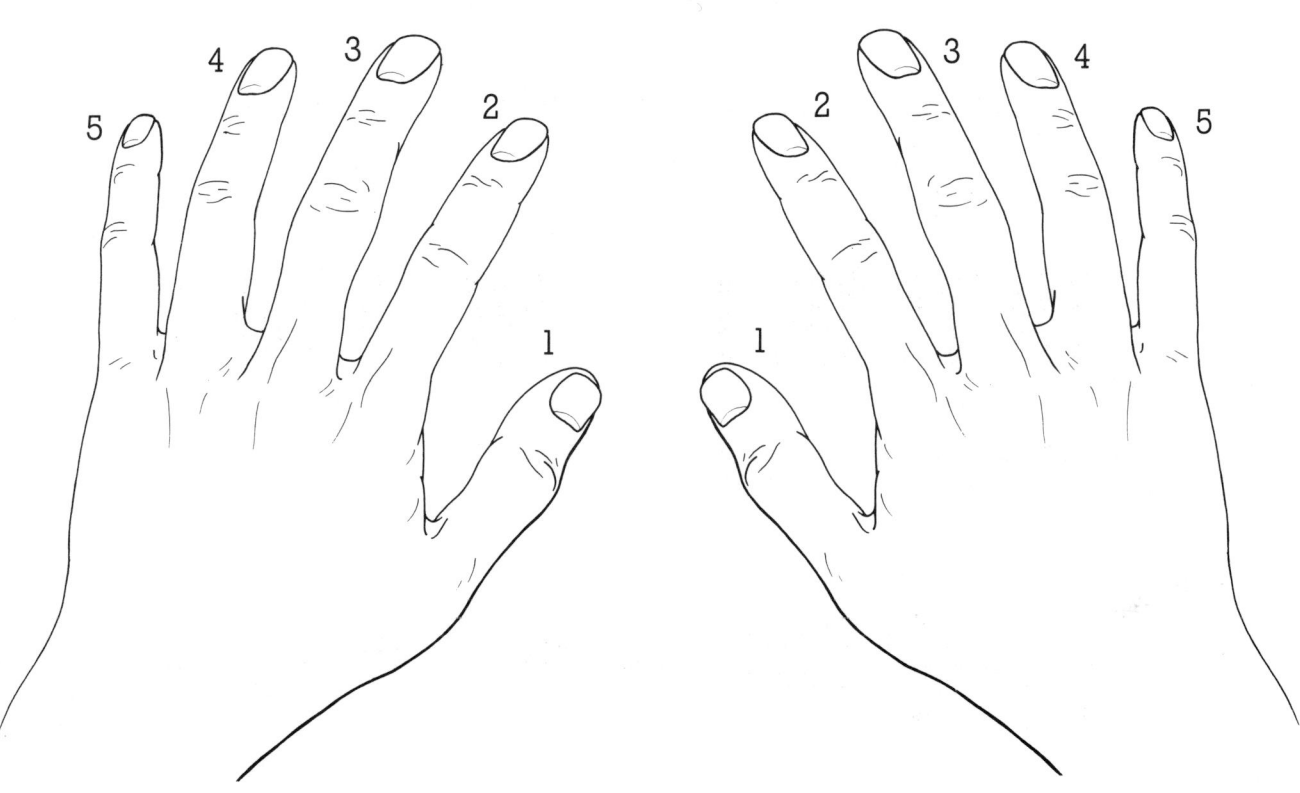

First Melody Notes

Here are your first five melody notes:

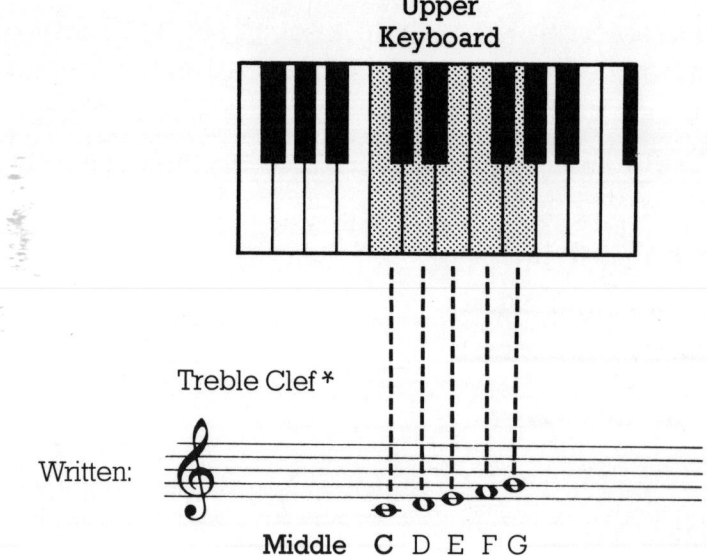

Play through the first four pieces in this book (up to and including 'Barcarolle') with your right hand alone on the Upper Keyboard, just to get the idea. I have written in the Letter Names of the notes to help you.

FOLLOW THE LETTER NAMES, NOT THE FINGERING.

First Two Chords

These chords, C and G7, are played by your left hand on the Lower Keyboard:

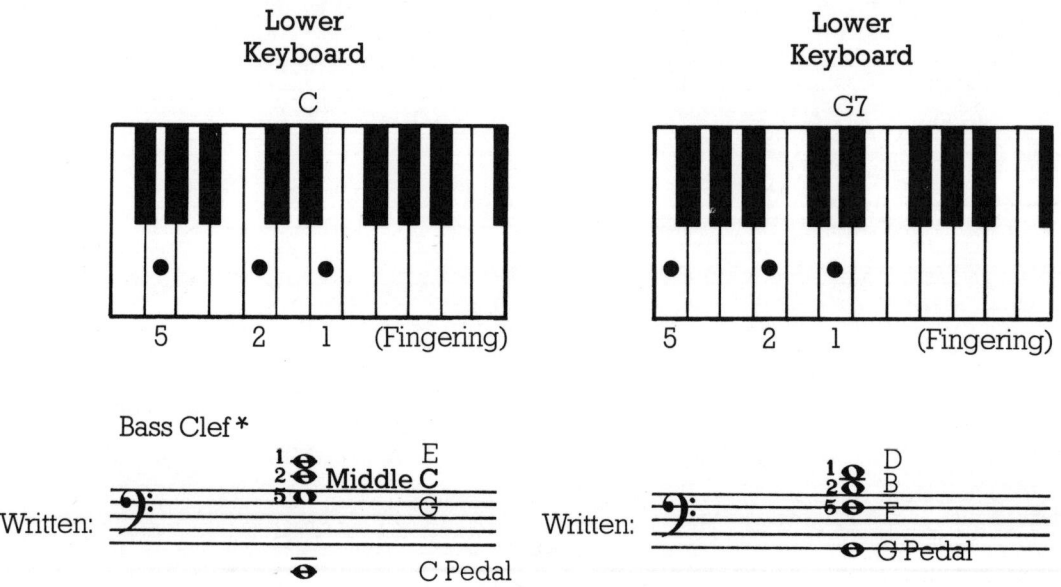

* See Dictionary of Musical Terms, p.45

Pedals

With the C Chord play C Pedal (either of the two C Pedals will do, but play the lower one for the moment).

With the G7 Chord play G Pedal.

Chord Practice

Practise moving from C Chord to G7 Chord and back. Always include pedals, since the pedal notes are an integral part of the chords. Play through the first four pieces (up to and including 'Barcarolle') using left hand and pedals only.

When you are reasonably proficient with the chords and pedals play through the same four pieces again and include the Melody (right hand).

Musical Timing

In most songs there is a regularly recurring pulse, or beat. The basic pulse notes are usually written like this:

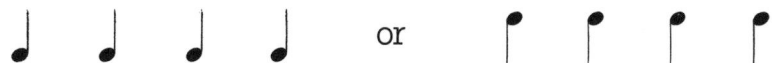

These are called Crotchets (or Quarter Notes).

Small vertical lines divide the songs up into 'bars,' or 'measures.'

Each bar contains the same number of crotchets (or their equivalent). As an example, let's look ahead to 'Jingle Bells,' on page 14:

Jingle Bells (p. 14)

In this short extract each bar has four beats, written as crotchets (quarter notes). This is indicated at the beginning by the Time Signature: $\frac{4}{4}$. This tells you that there are 4 'quarter' notes (or their equivalent) in each bar. $\frac{3}{4}$ would tell you that there are 3 'quarter' notes in each bar, and so on.

Play through the above example (right hand only), keeping a steady pulse throughout. All your crotchets must be exactly the same length.

Other Time Notes

In the short extract from 'Jingle Bells' which you just played, the melody consisted entirely of crotchets. If you look at the rest of the song (p. 14), you will see several other time notes being used. Here are the values of these time notes:

time note	name	lasting
♩ or ♩	crotchet (quarter note)	1 beat (or count)
♩ or ♩	minim (half note)	2 beats (or counts)
♩. or ♩.	dotted minim (dotted half note)	3 beats (or counts)
o	semibreve (whole note)	4 beats (or counts)

Here's how you apply the longer time notes:

Jingle Bells (p. 14)

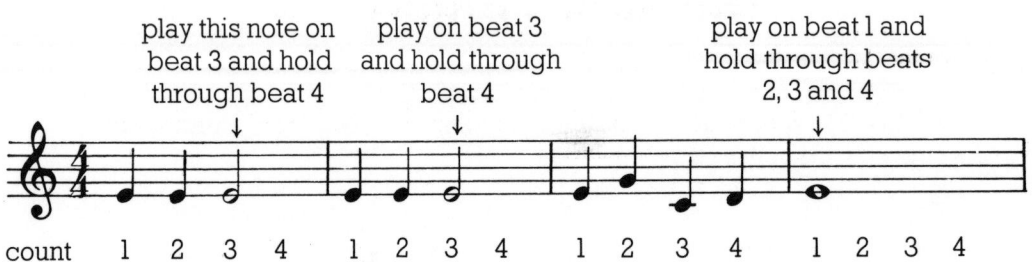

Play the above example through a few times. Be sure to keep to a regular pulse. When you are happy with it, turn to page 14 and play the whole of 'Jingle Bells' through (right hand only).

Next learn the new chord required (F6), and add the left hand and pedals to 'Jingle Bells.'

Now go back over the first four pieces in the book, this time keeping to a regular pulse and counting out your long notes correctly. You could try adding your rhythm unit at this stage, to see how accurate you are.

You will see that 'Barcarolle' (p. 13) has three beats to the bar, not four. Don't let this throw you: the principle of counting beats is exactly the same.

Merrily We Roll Along
Traditional

Upper: piano (with sustain)
Lower: flutes (with tremolo)
Pedal: 16' + 8'

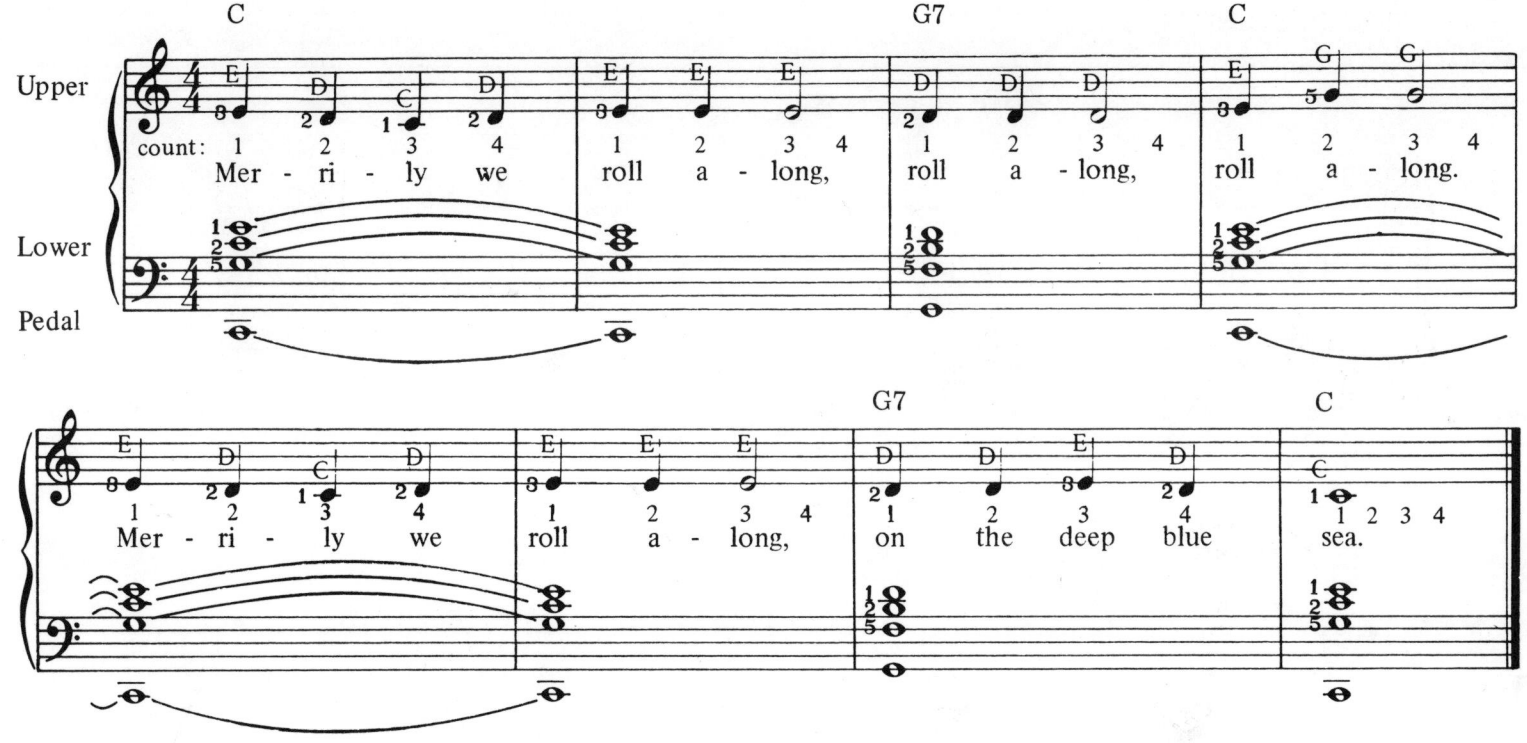

Largo
Dvořák

Upper: oboe (with small vibrato)
Lower: strings (with sustain)
Pedal: 8'

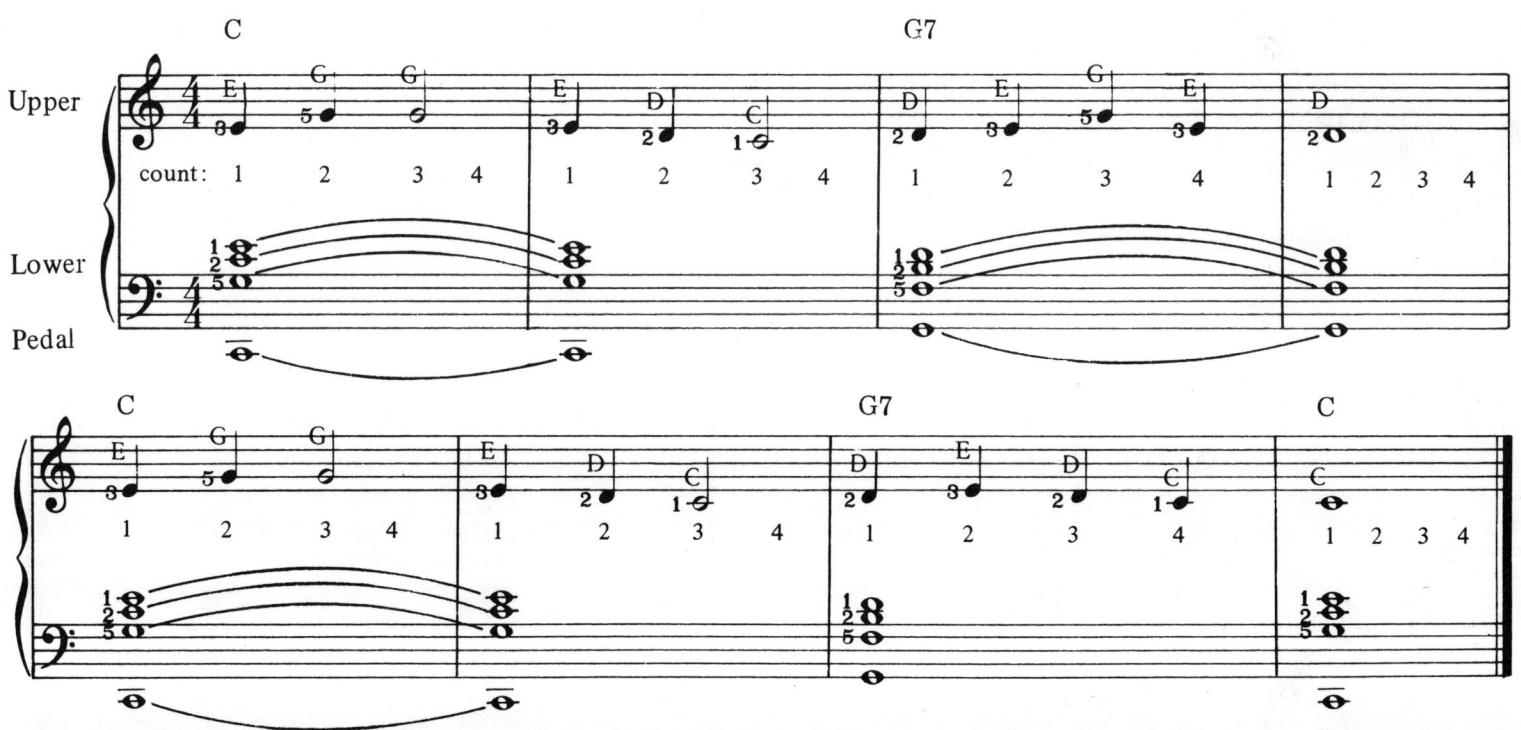

Lightly Row
Traditional

Upper: saxophone (with vibrato)
Lower: flutes (with tremolo)
Pedal: 16' + 8'

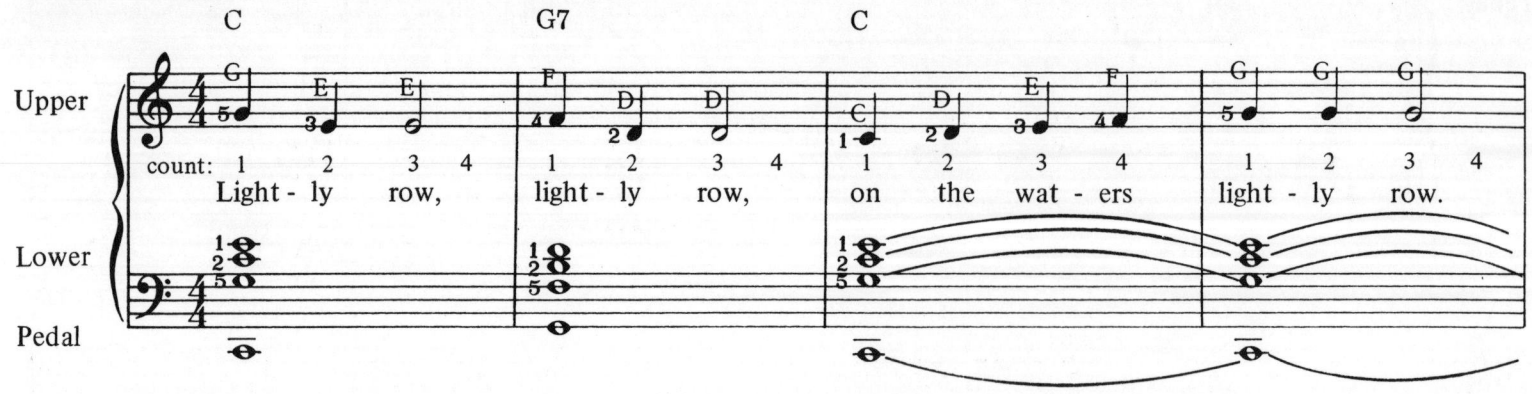

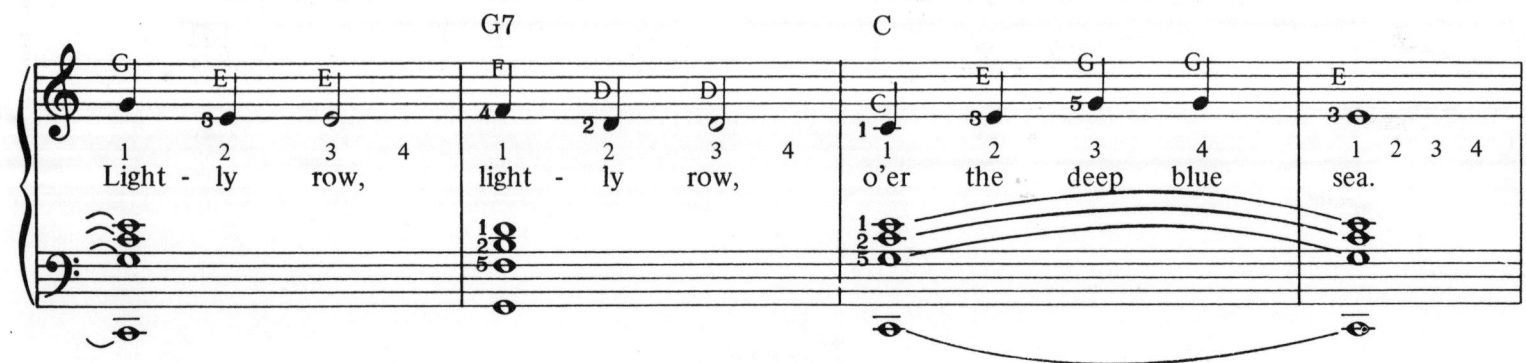

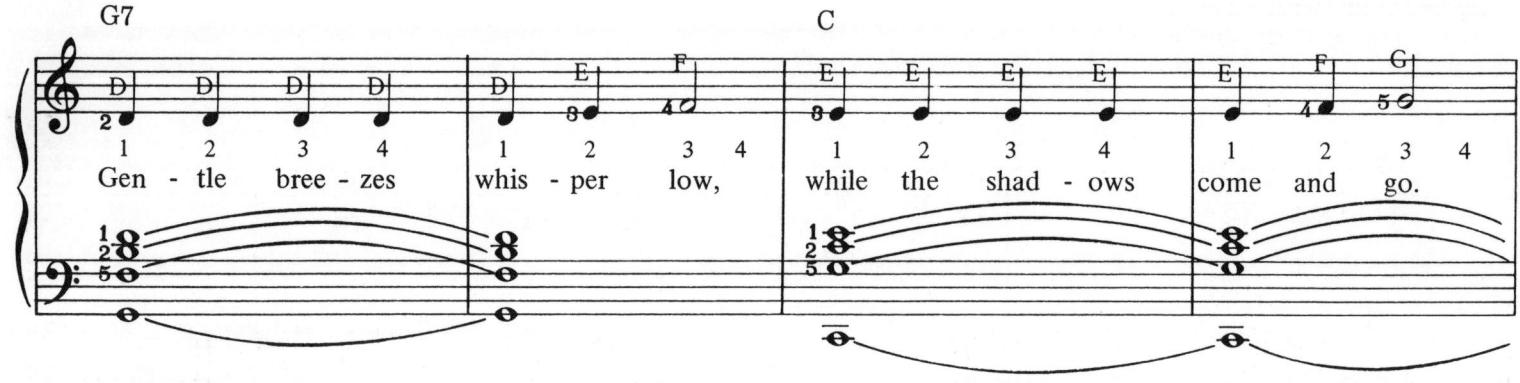

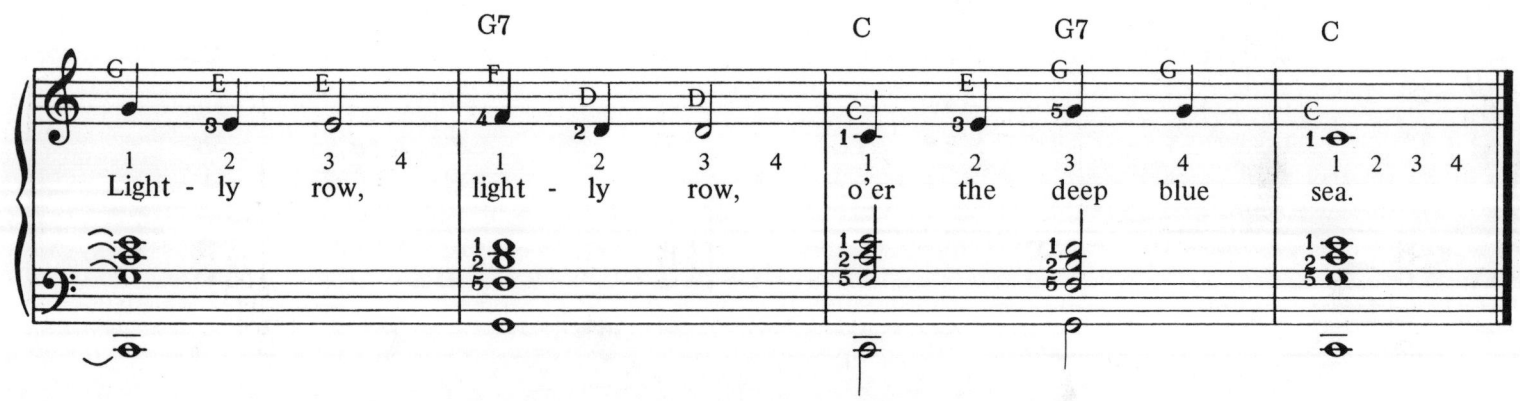

© Copyright 1977 by Dorsey Bros. Music Ltd., 8/9 Frith Street, London W1V 5TZ.
All Rights Reserved. International Copyright Secured.

Barcarolle
Offenbach

Upper: **string ensemble** (with sustain)
Lower: **flutes** (with tremolo)
Pedal: 16′

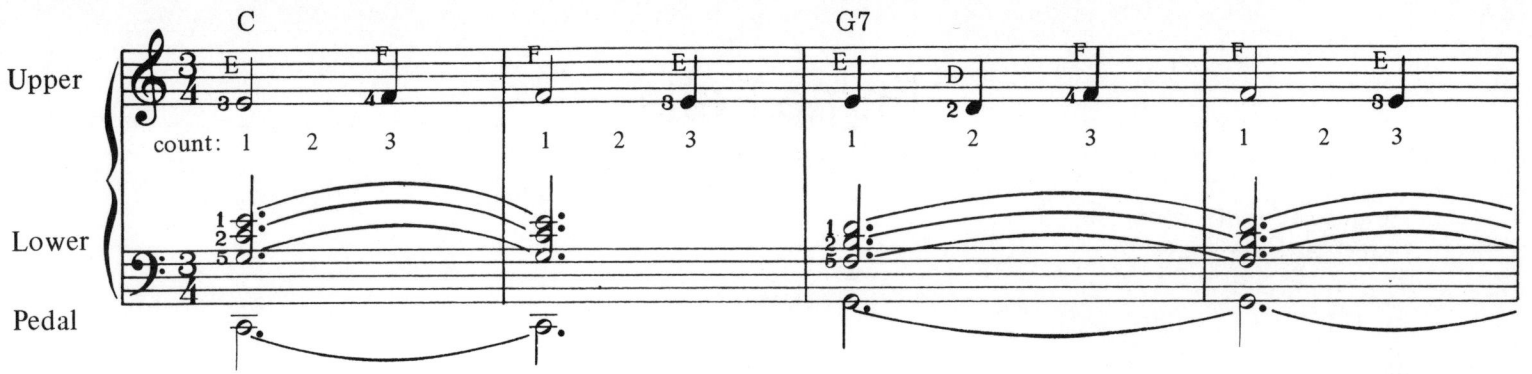
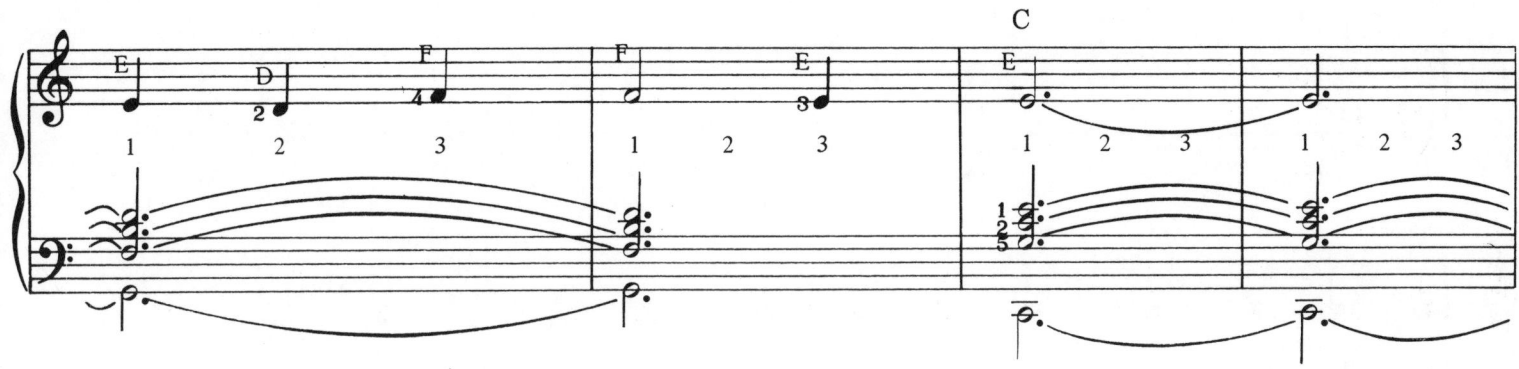
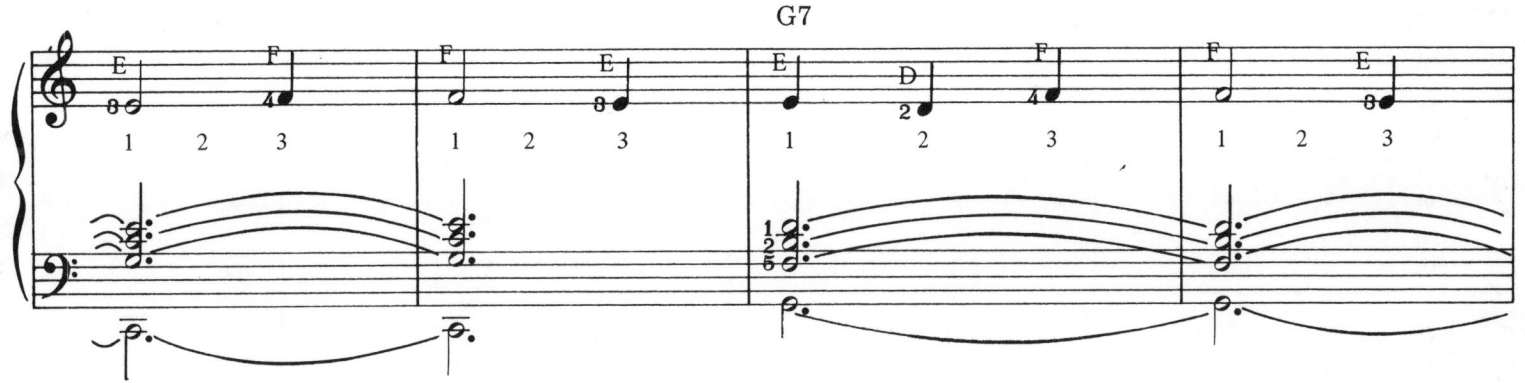
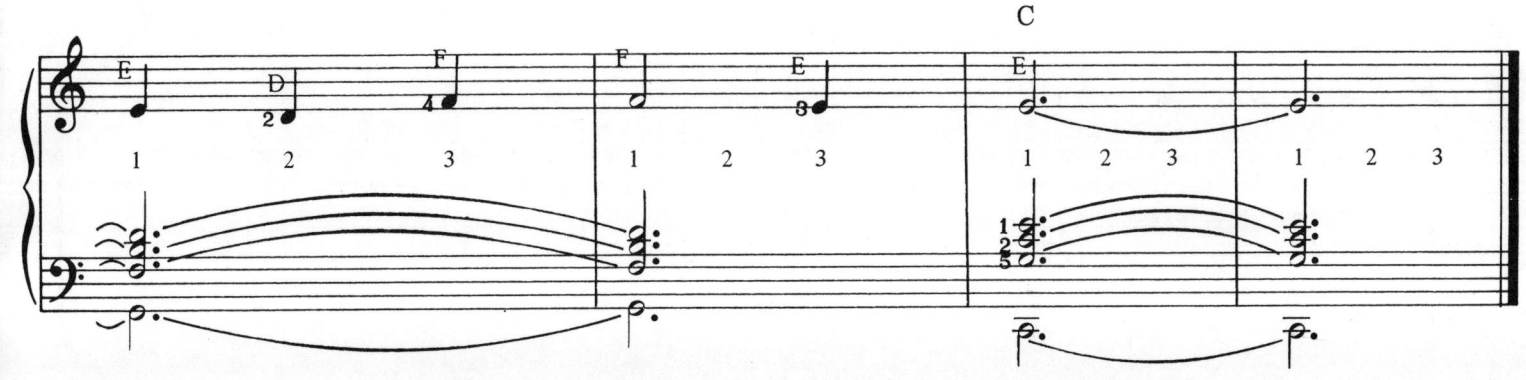

New Chord: F6

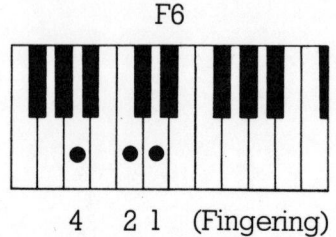

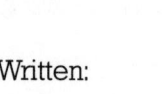

F6

4 2 1 (Fingering)

Written:

F6

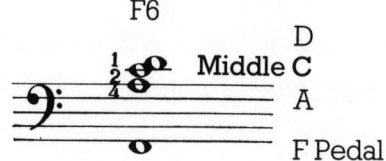

Jingle Bells

Pierpont

Upper: vibraphone (with sustain)
Lower: flutes (with tremolo)
Pedal: 8′

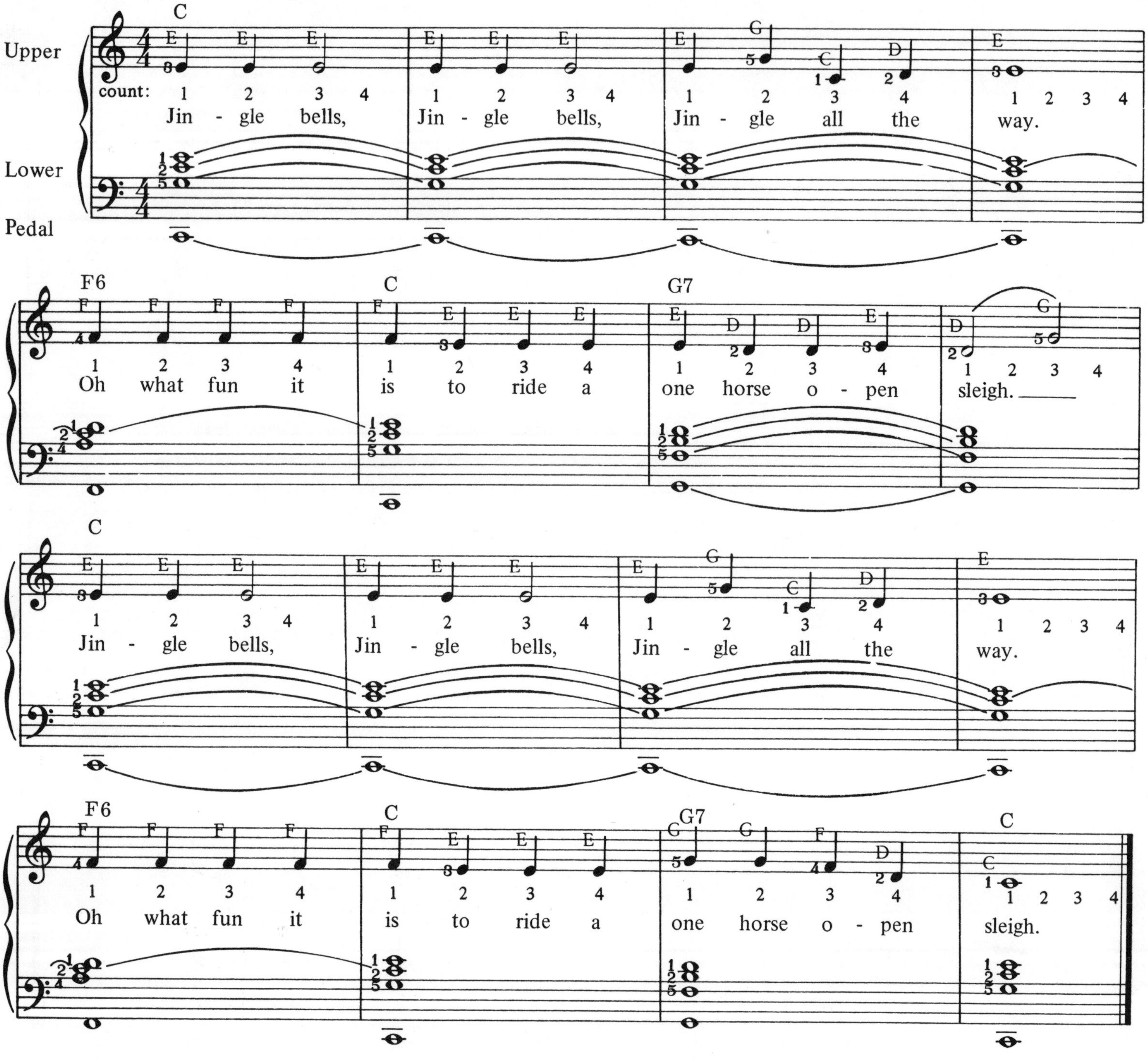

Ties

When a note is to sing for more than four beats it is 'tied' to a note of the appropriate length in the next bar:

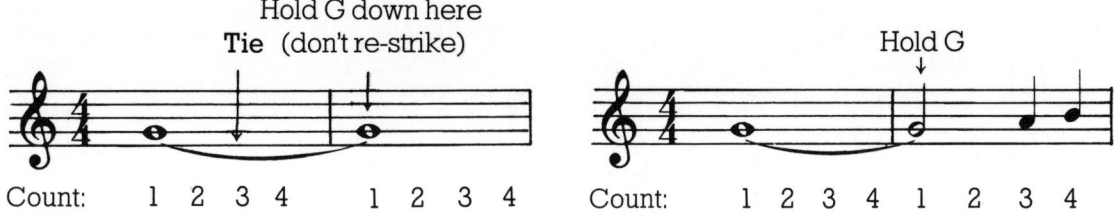

Let this note G sing for a total of 8 beats.　　Let this note G sing for a total of 6 beats, then move on to note A.

Look out for 'ties' in your right hand in the next piece: 'When The Saints Go Marching In' (p. 16). If you look back at your earlier pieces, you will see ties in the left hand and pedals.

Rests

Periods of silence during a piece are written as 'rests:'

- 𝄽   crotchet (quarter note) rest. A silence lasting for 1 beat.
- 𝄼   minim (half note) rest. A silence lasting for 2 beats.
- 𝄼·   dotted minim (dotted half note) rest. A silence lasting for 3 beats.
- 𝄻   semibreve (whole note) rest. A silence lasting for 4 beats. This rest can also signify one whole bar's rest (regardless of how many beats per bar).

Look out for 'rests' (specially in the left hand and pedals) in the pieces which follow.

Pick-Up Notes

Songs do not always begin on beat 1. Your next piece, 'When The Saints Go Marching In,' starts on beat 2, and there are two more preliminary 'pick up' notes before the first beat 1.

IN TUNES WITH PICK UP NOTES AT THE BEGINNING, THE FIRST CHORD DOESN'T USUALLY APPEAR UNTIL THE FIRST BEAT 1.

When The Saints Go Marching In
New words & Music by Chris Barber

Upper: **flutes** 16' 8' 4' (88 0800 000) (with tremolo)
Lower: **strings** (with sustain)
Pedal: 16' + 8'

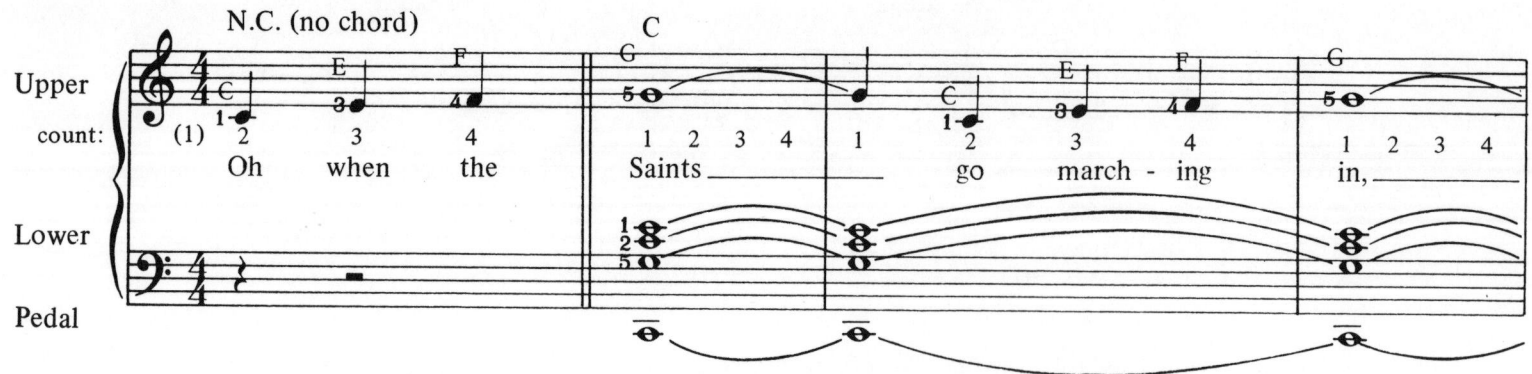
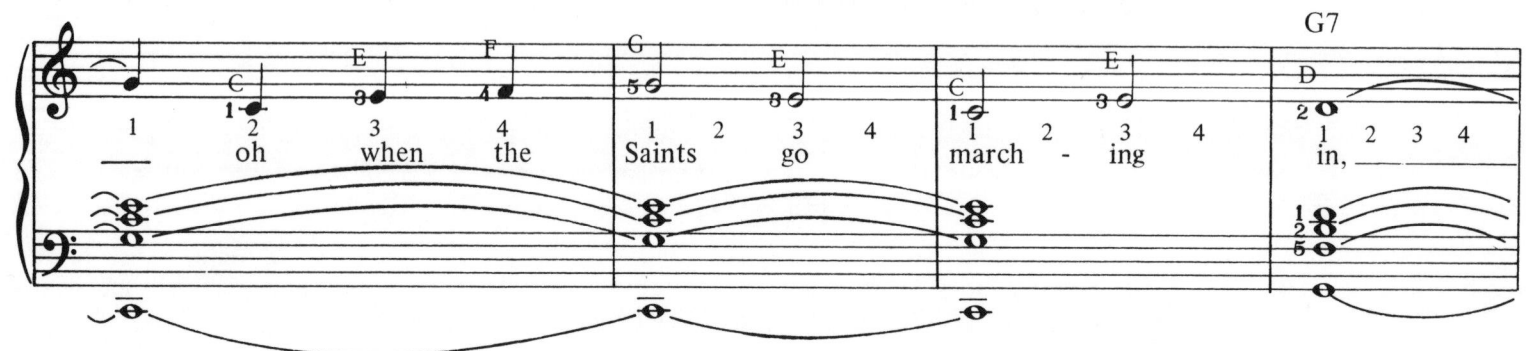
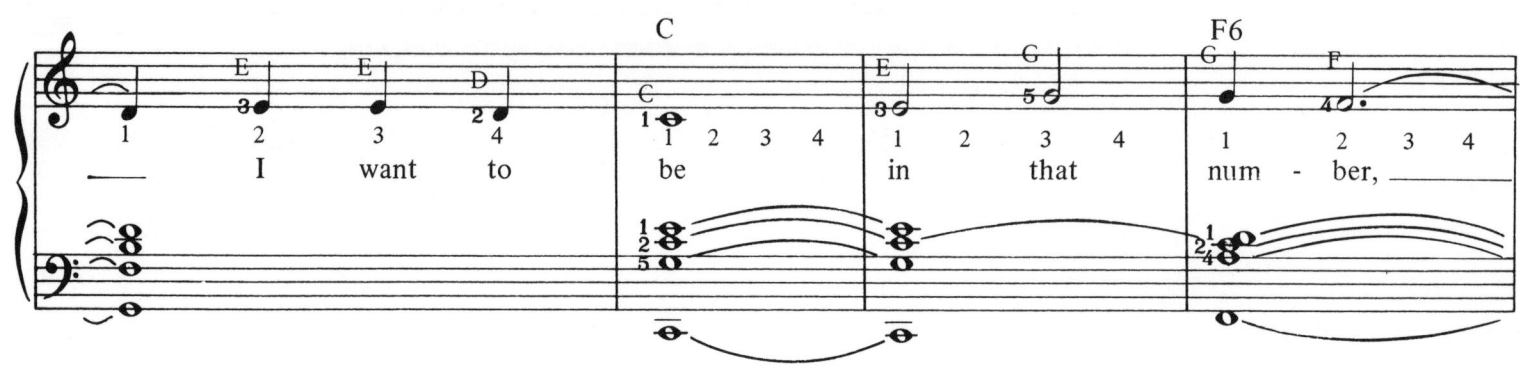
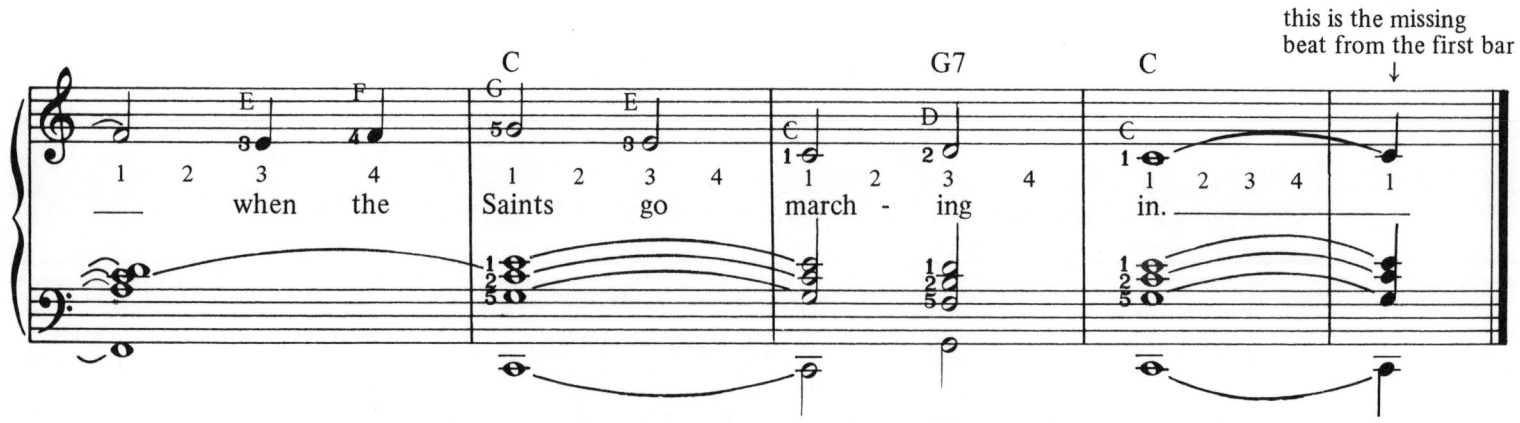

© Copyright 1977 by Dorsey Bros. Music Ltd., 8/9 Frith Street, London W1V 5TZ.
All Rights Reserved. International Copyright Secured.

New Melody Note: A

Written:

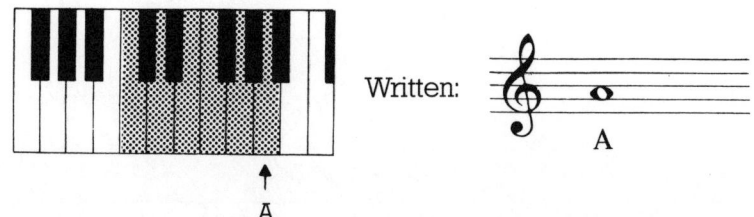

Michael Row The Boat Ashore

Traditional

Upper: clarinet (with, or without vibrato)
Lower: strings (with sustain)
Pedal: 8′

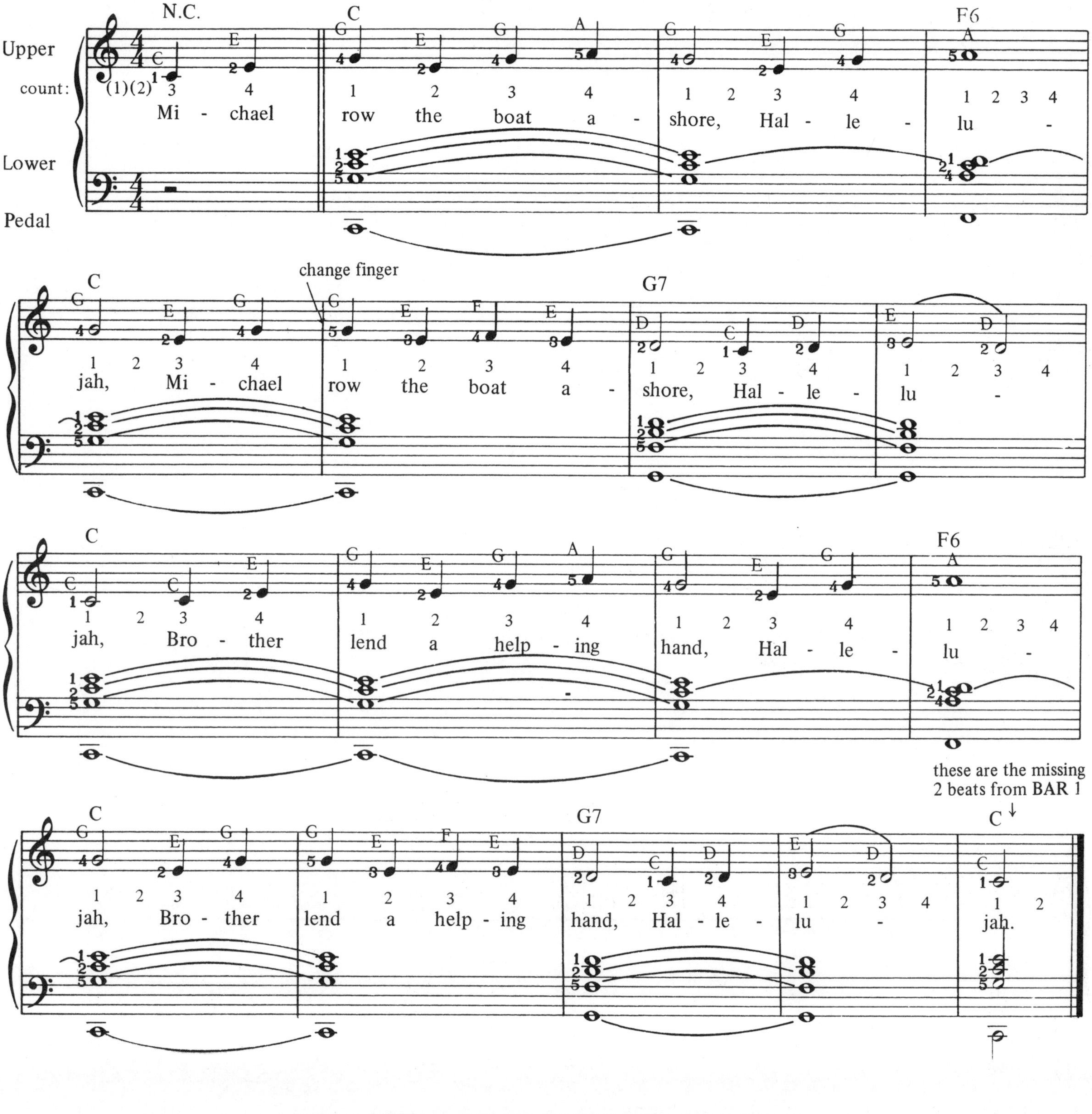

For He's A Jolly Good Fellow
Traditional

Upper: trombone (with vibrato)
Lower: flutes (with tremolo)
Pedal: 16' + 8'

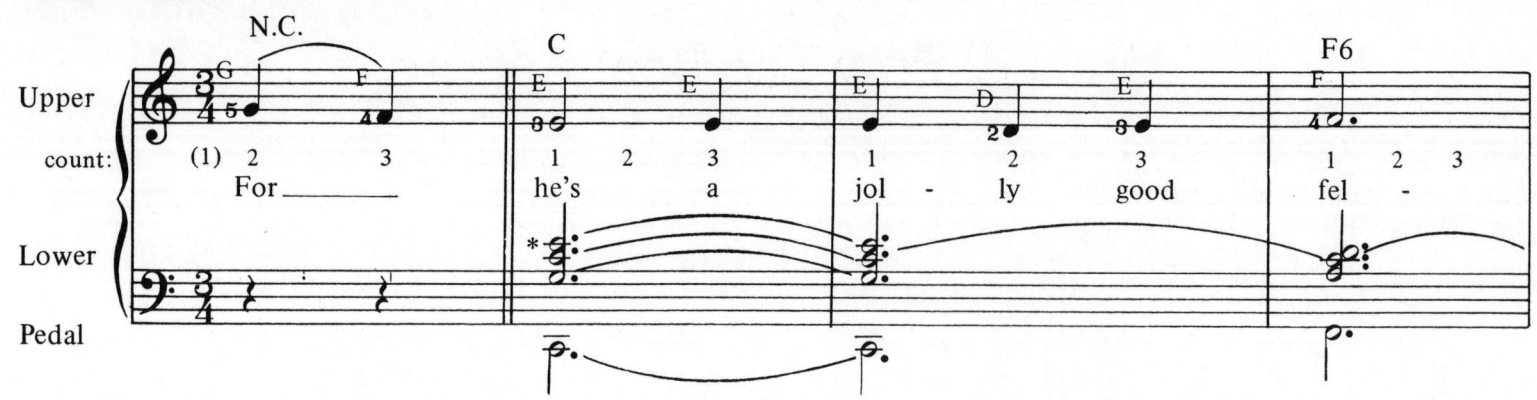
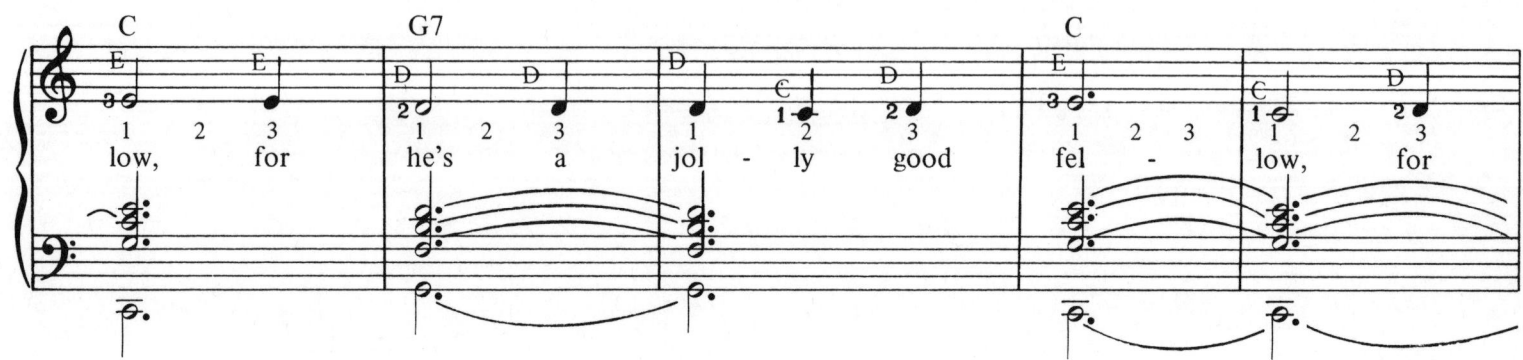
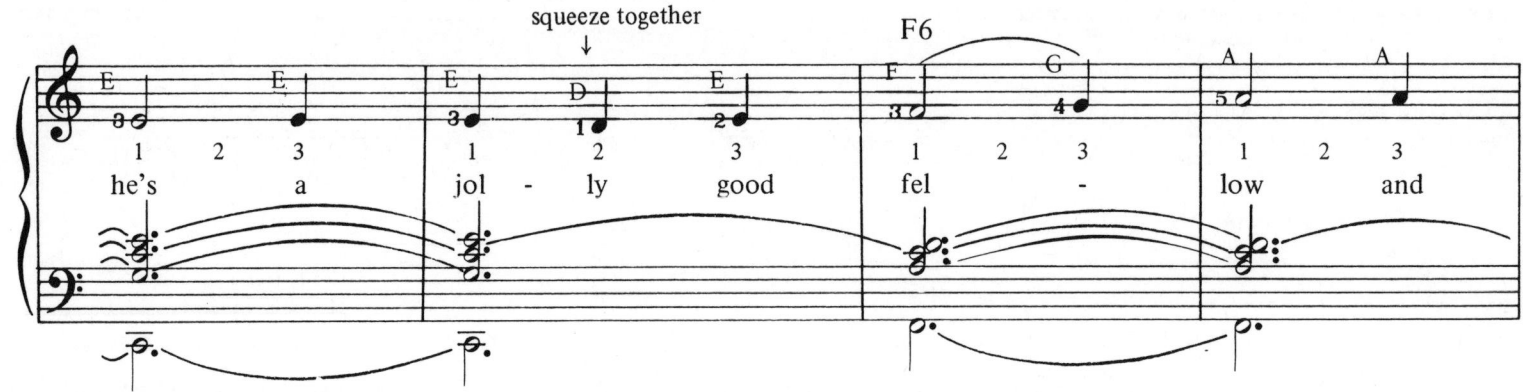
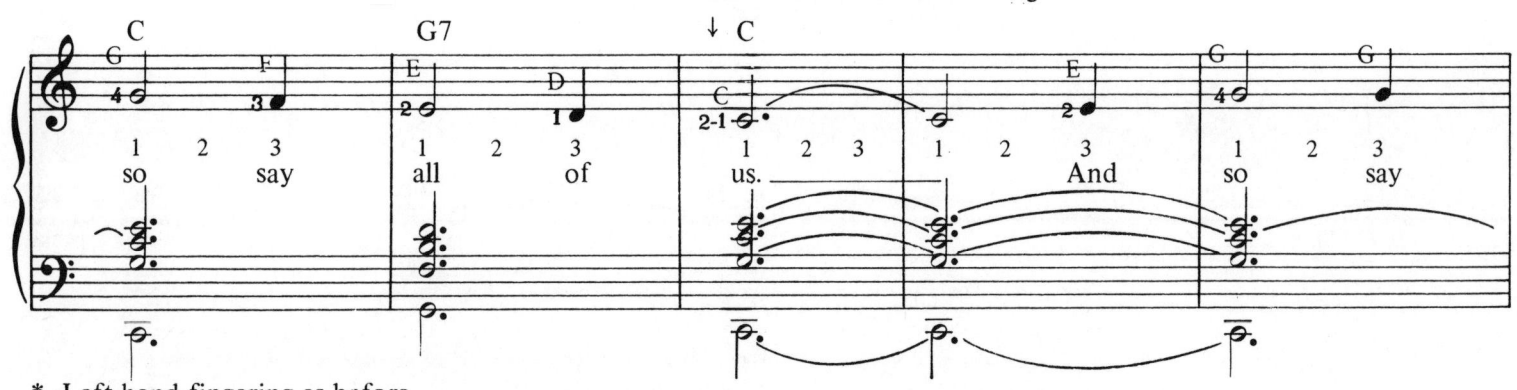

* Left hand fingering as before.

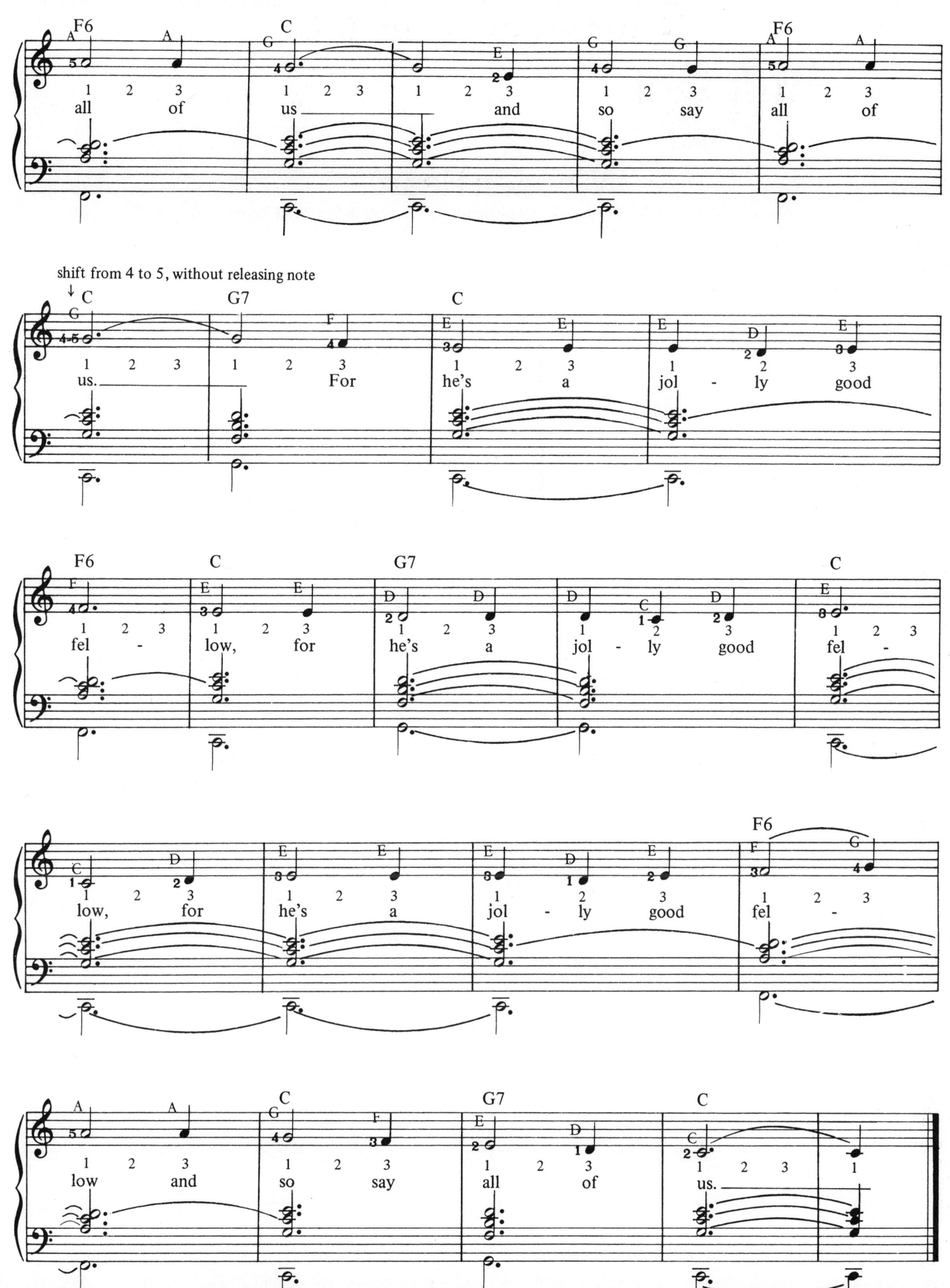

New Melody Notes: B, C

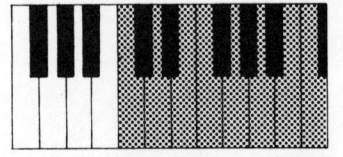

Written: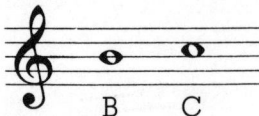

Wooden Heart

Words & Music by Fred Wise, Ben Weisman, Kay Twomey & Berthold Kaempfert

Upper: string ensemble + piano (with sustain)
Lower: flute (with tremolo)
Pedal: 16' + 8'

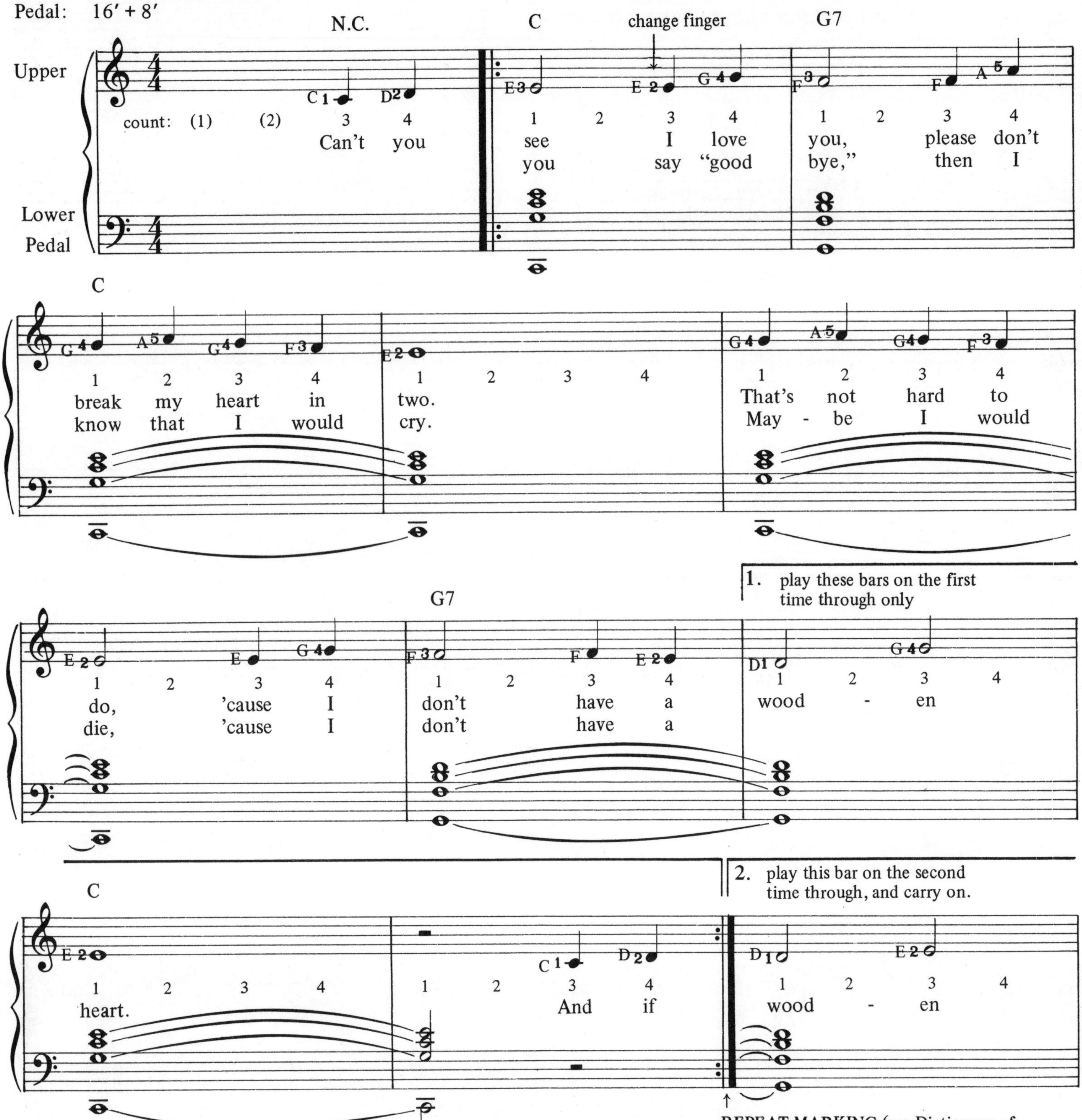

[Sheet music for "Wooden Heart" with lyrics:]

Can't you see I love you, please don't break my heart in two. / know that I would cry. That's not hard to May-be I would do, 'cause I don't have a wood-en die, 'cause I don't have a

1. play these bars on the first time through only

heart. And if

2. play this bar on the second time through, and carry on.

wood-en

REPEAT MARKING (see Dictionary of Musical Terms, p. 45)

© Copyright 1960 Gladys Music Inc., New York, USA.
Carlin Music Corp., 14 New Burlington St., London W1 for the territory of
United Kingdom of Great Britain & Northern Ireland, Eire, Israel and the British Dominions, Colonies,
Overseas Territories & Dependencies (excluding Canada, Australia & New Zealand).
All Rights Reserved. International Copyright Secured.

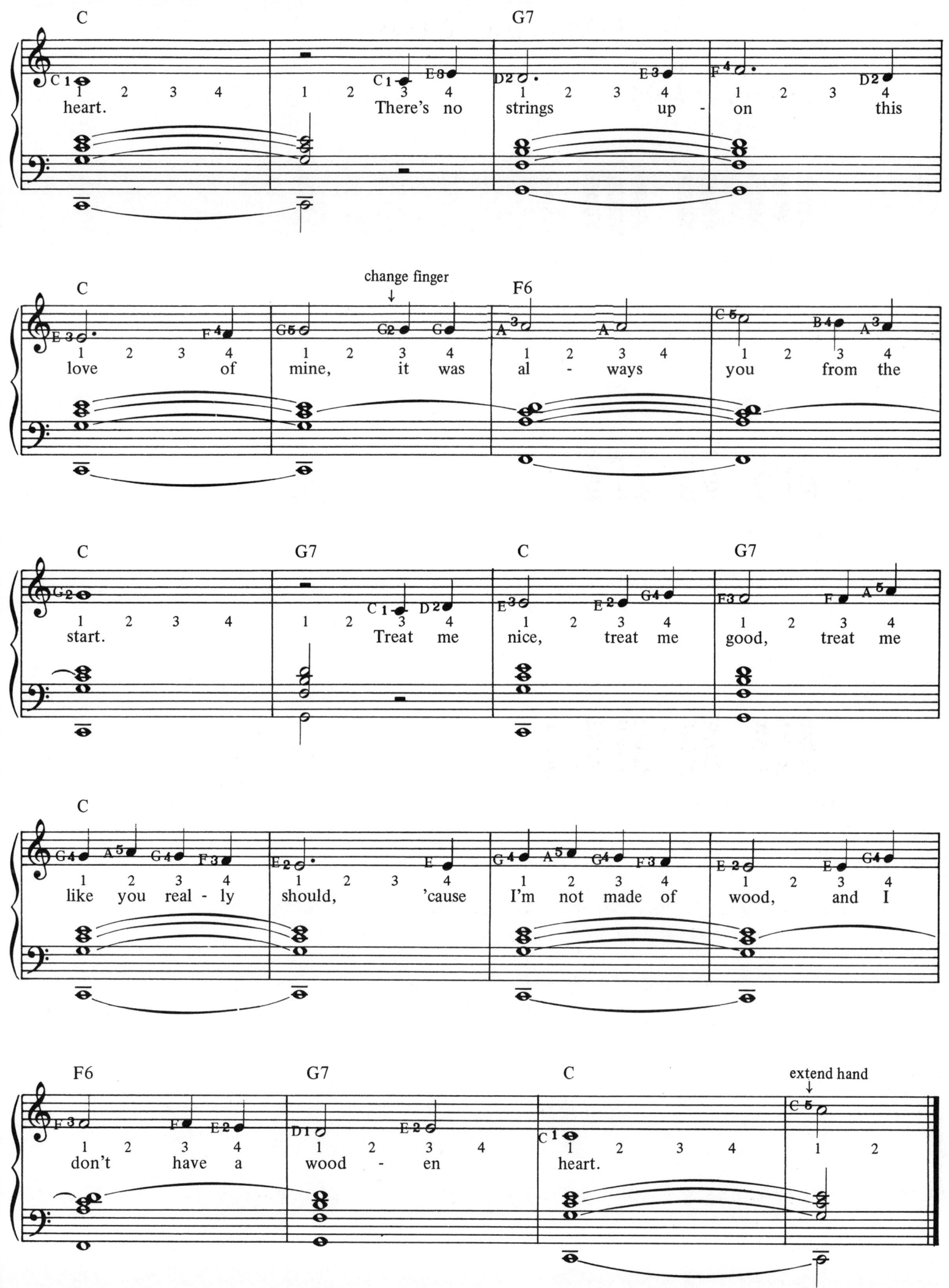

Four-Note Chords

By adding a fourth note to each of your three basic chords you get a richer, fuller sound:

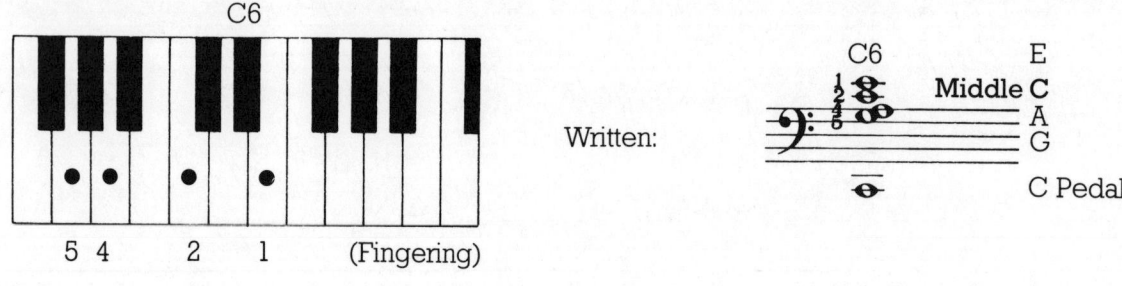

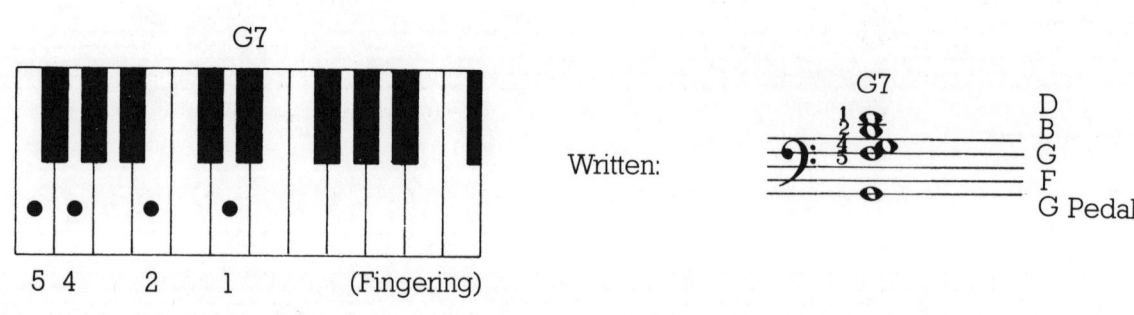

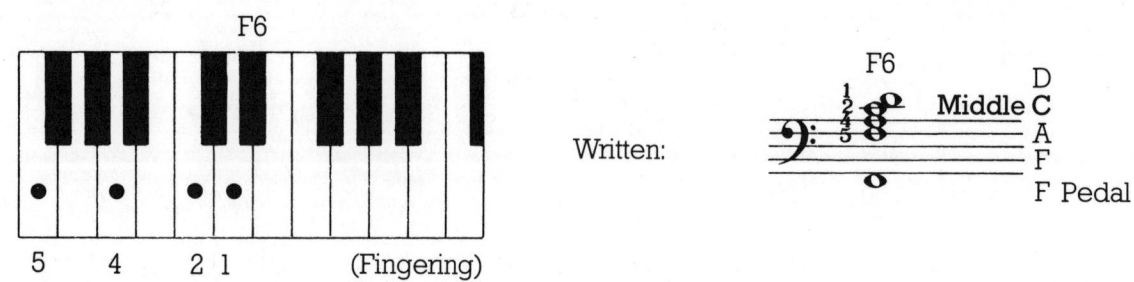

You will find four-note chords very little harder to learn and play than three-note chords, and they will prove well worth the extra effort.

Observe the fingering carefully, and in the musical examples that follow observe the 'tied' notes (e.g. if C and A are together like this:-

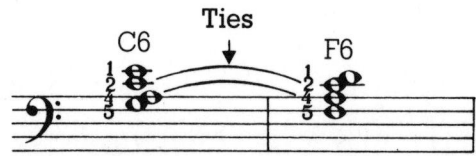

hold fingers 2 and 4 down whilst fingers 1 and 5 move to their new notes). The result will be a smoother transition from chord to chord, and in the end will be easiest to do.

New Melody Notes: D, E, F

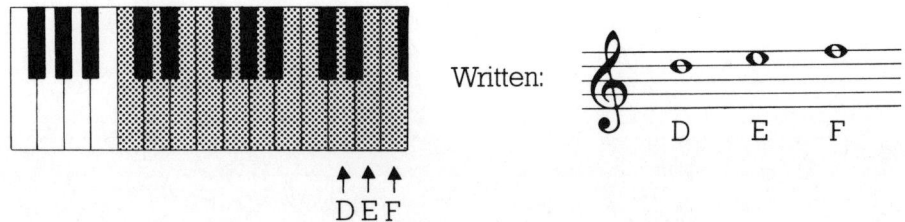

From now on only new letter names will be used against the notes.

Love Me Tender

Words & Music by Elvis Presley and Vera Matson

Upper: flute (with vibrato)
Lower: strings (with sustain)
Pedal: 8′

© Copyright 1956 by Elvis Presley Music Inc., New York, USA.
Carlin Music Corp., 14 New Burlington Street, London W1. For the British Empire (excluding Canada, Australasia, New Zealand and South Africa) and the Republic of Ireland.
All Rights Reserved. International Copyright Secured.

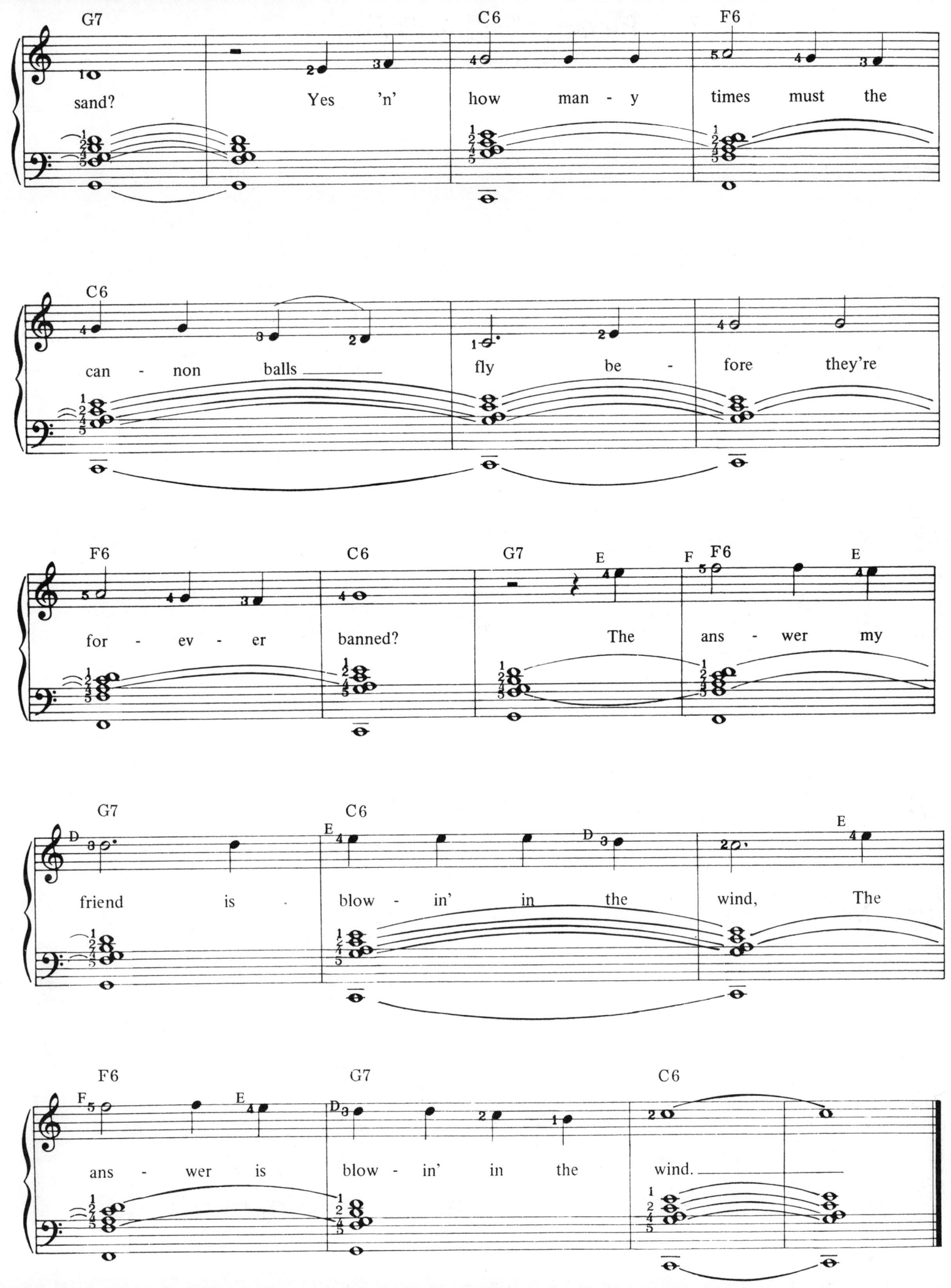

Eight Days A Week
Words & Music by John Lennon & Paul McCartney

Upper: jazz guitar
Lower: flutes (with tremolo)
Pedal: 8′

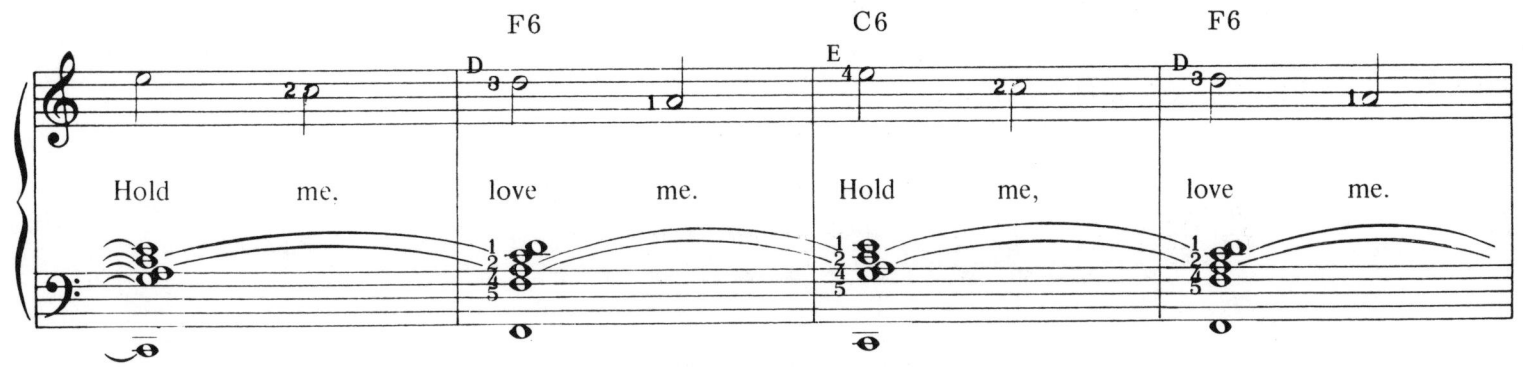

© Copyright 1964 for the World by Northern Songs Ltd., 3/5 Rathbone Place, London W1.
All Rights Reserved. International Copyright Secured.

The Beginnings of Rhythmic Playing

A simple way to bring out the rhythm in your pieces is to strike a pedal note at the beginning of every bar – even when the chord doesn't change.

Use your Rhythm Unit from now on: it will not only fill out the rhythm, it will help you keep time. From now on I have given suggested drum rhythms, and metronome* markings, indicating tempo (speed).

New Melody Note: G

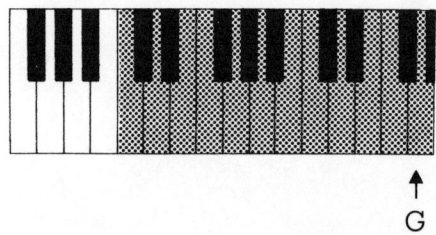

Written:

Quavers (Eighth Notes): ♪ or ♫   ♫ or ♫

A Quaver (or Eighth Note) is a time note which is played twice as fast as the basic crotchet beat:

♩ = ♫

crotchet (1 beat) = quavers (two 'half' beats)

If you say the word 'and' between beat numbers, you will get the exact timing of the quaver.

Play the following exercises:

Exercise 1

Exercise 2: Skip To My Lou (p. 29)

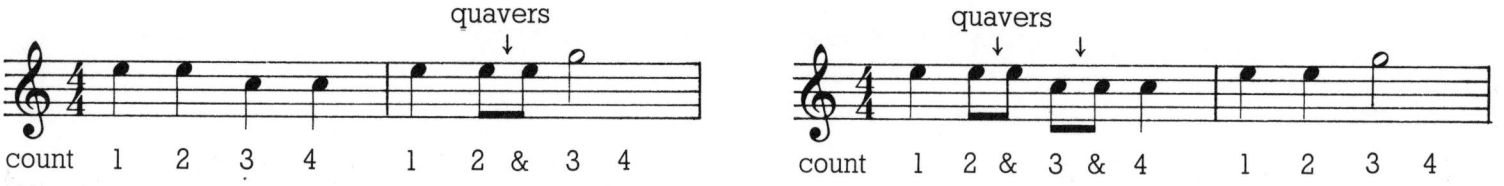

Quaver (Eighth) Rest: 𝄾

This sign denotes a silence equal to one quaver (half a beat).

*See Dictionary of Musical Terms, p.45

Skip To My Lou

Traditional

Upper: vibraphone (with sustain)
Lower: **flutes** (with tremolo)
Pedal: 8′
Drums: march (2/4) ♩ = 108

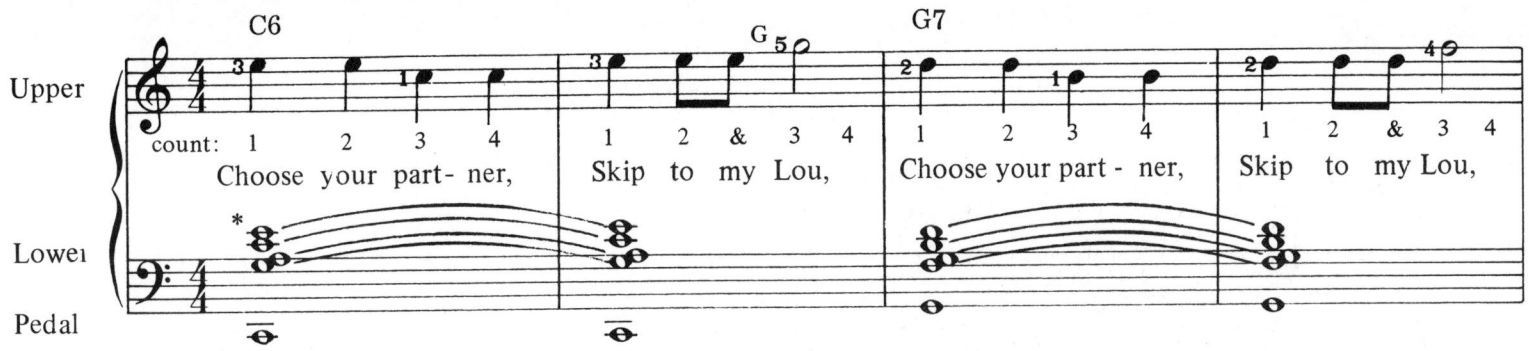

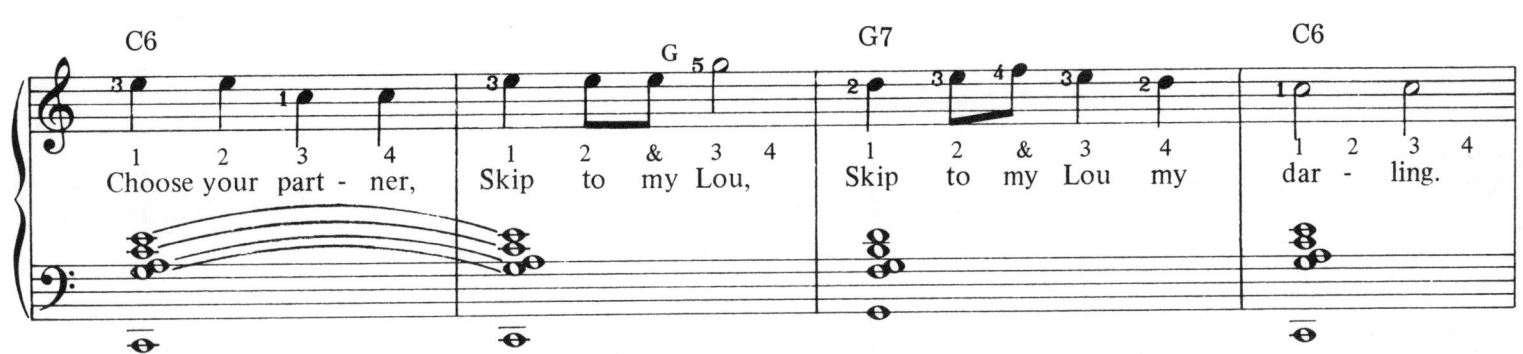

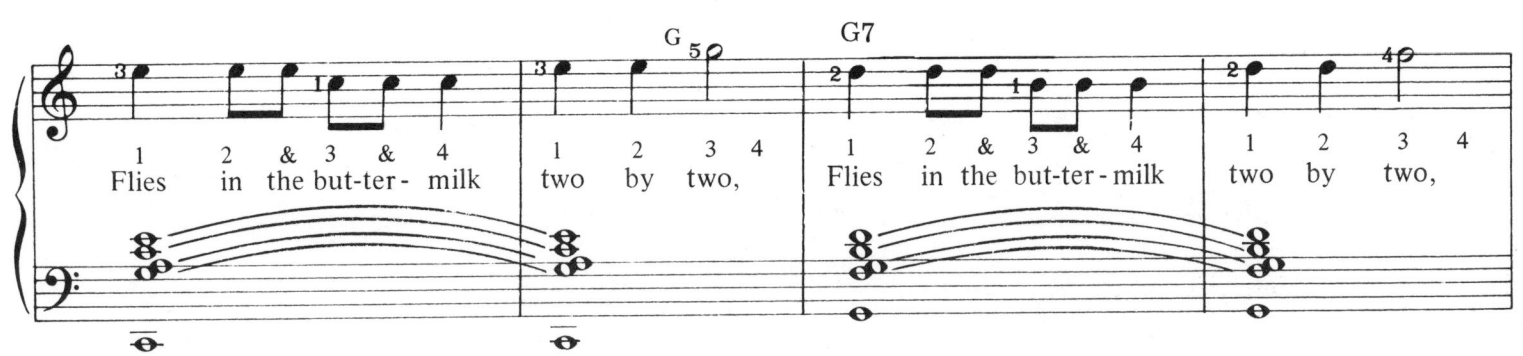

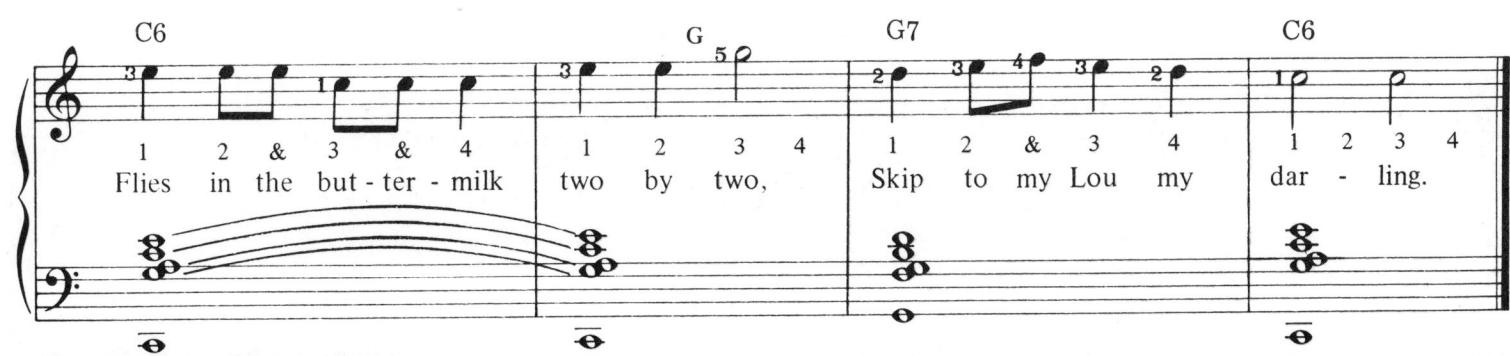

* Left hand fingering as before

© Copyright 1977 by Dorsey Bros. Music Ltd., 8/9 Frith Street, London W1V 5TZ.
All Rights Reserved. International Copyright Secured.

Super Trouper

Words & Music by Benny Andersson & Bjorn Ulvaeus

Upper: jazz guitar + flutes (with tremolo)
Lower: flutes (with tremolo)
Pedal: bass guitar 8'
Drums: rock ♩ = 120

© Copyright 1980 Union Songs AB, Stockholm, Sweden for the World.
Bocu Music Ltd., 1 Wyndham Yard, Wyndham Place, London W1 for Great Britain and Eire.
All Rights Reserved. International Copyright Secured.

New Melody Note: High A

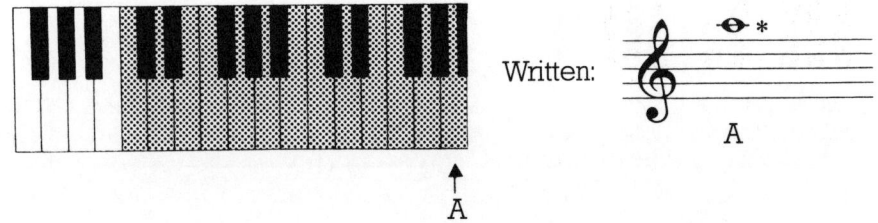

Gonna Build A Mountain
Words & Music by Anthony Newly & Leslie Bricusse

Upper: **flutes** 16′ 8′ 4′ (88 0006 0008) (with tremolo)
Lower: **flutes** (with tremolo)
Pedal: 8′
Drums: rock ♩ = 120

* 'Ledger Line', see Dictionary Of Musical Terms (p. 45)

© Copyright 1961 Tro-Essex Music Ltd., 19/20 Poland Street, London W1.
All Rights Reserved. International Copyright Secured.

New Chords: Am7, D7

Am7*

5 4 2 1 (Fingering)

Am7

Written:

D7

5 4 2 1 (Fingering)

D7

Written:

Every Breath You Take

Words & Music by Sting

Upper: jazz guitar
Lower: flutes (with tremolo)
Pedal: 16′ + 8′

Drums: rock ♩ = 100

* same as C6, except for the pedal note

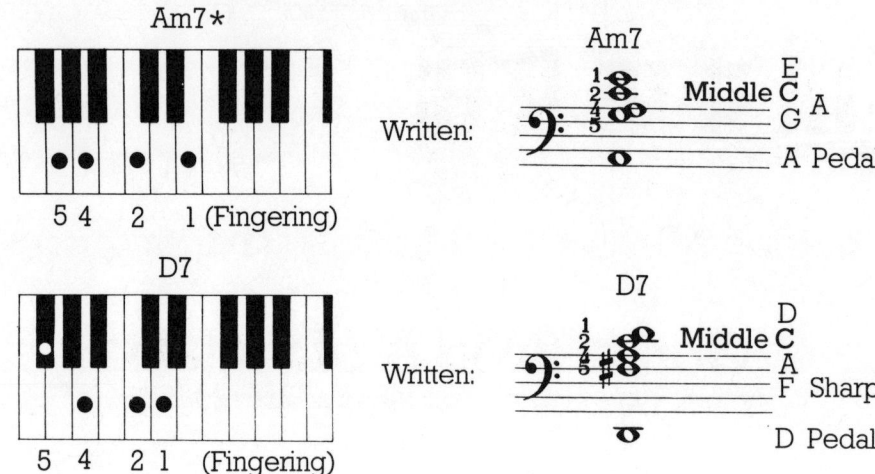

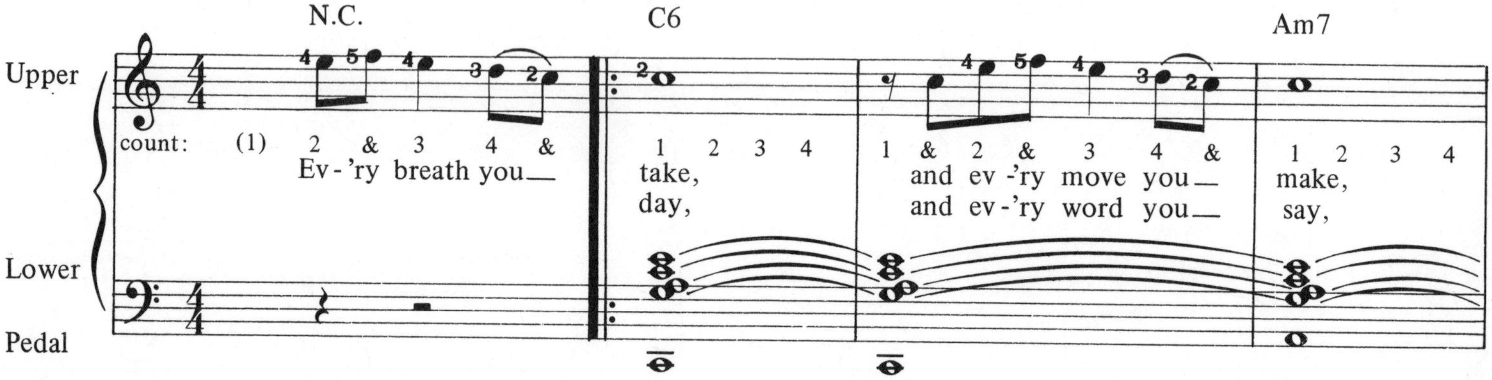

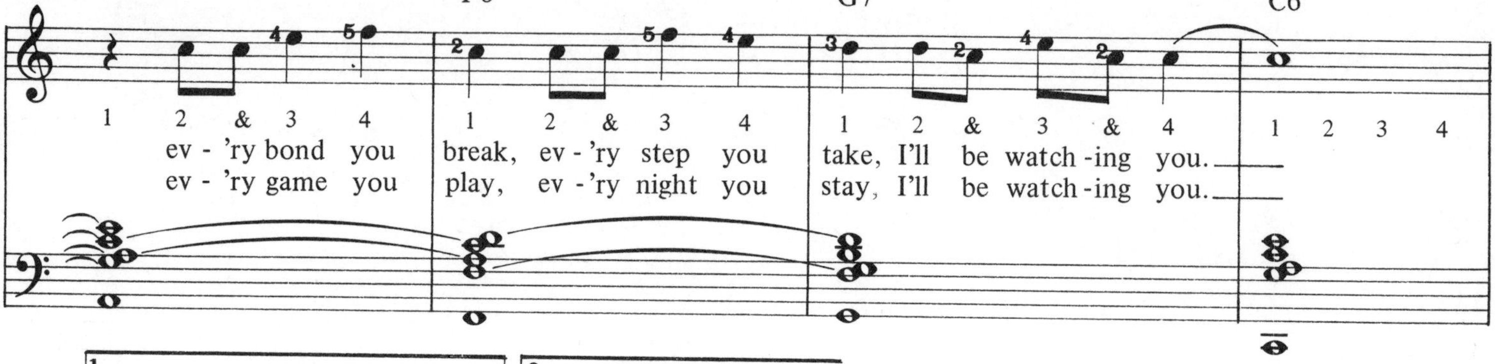

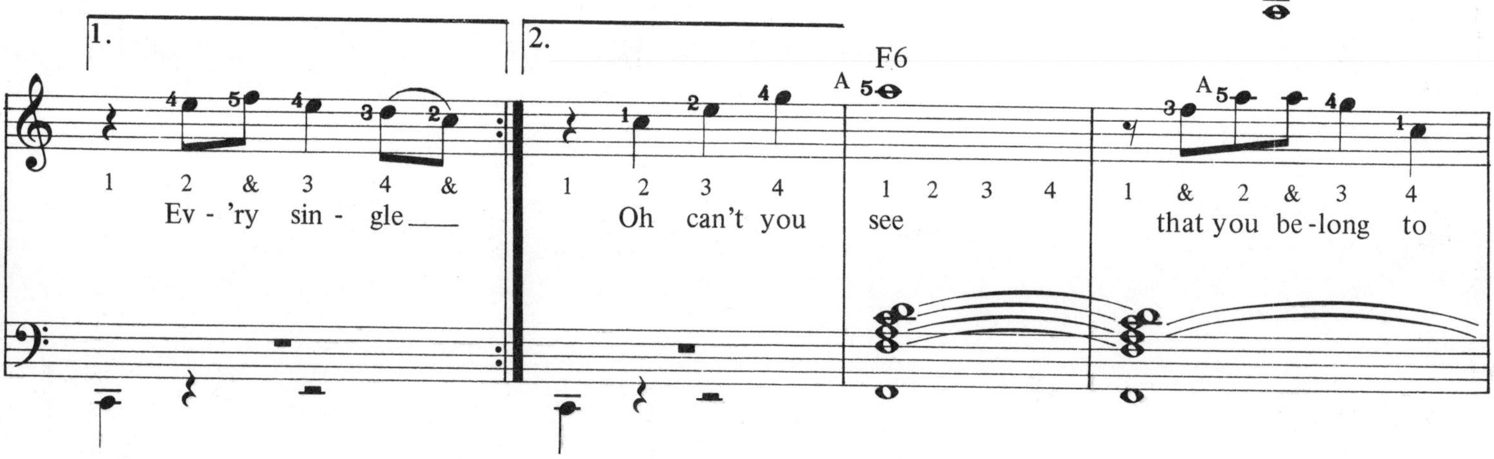

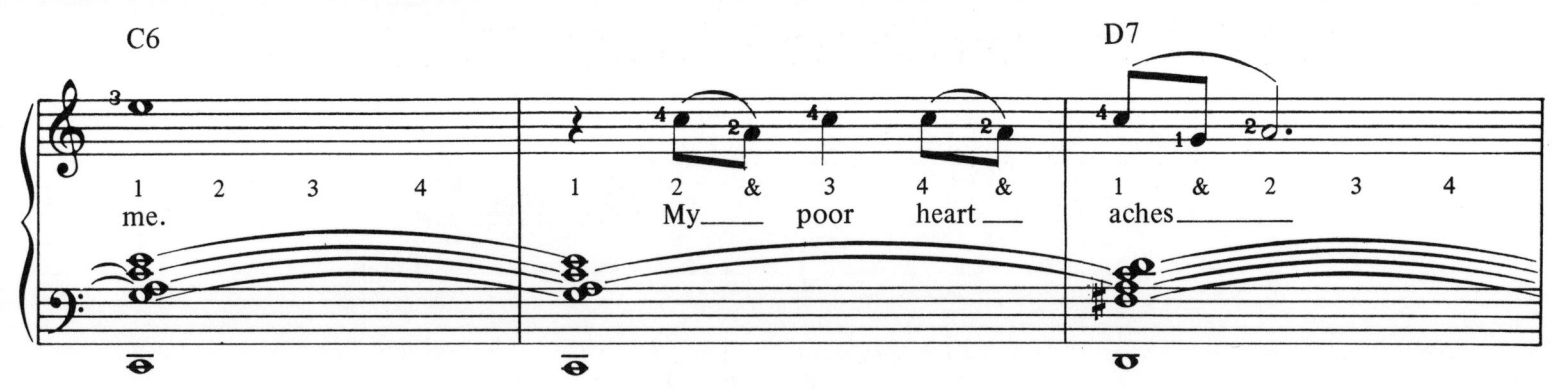
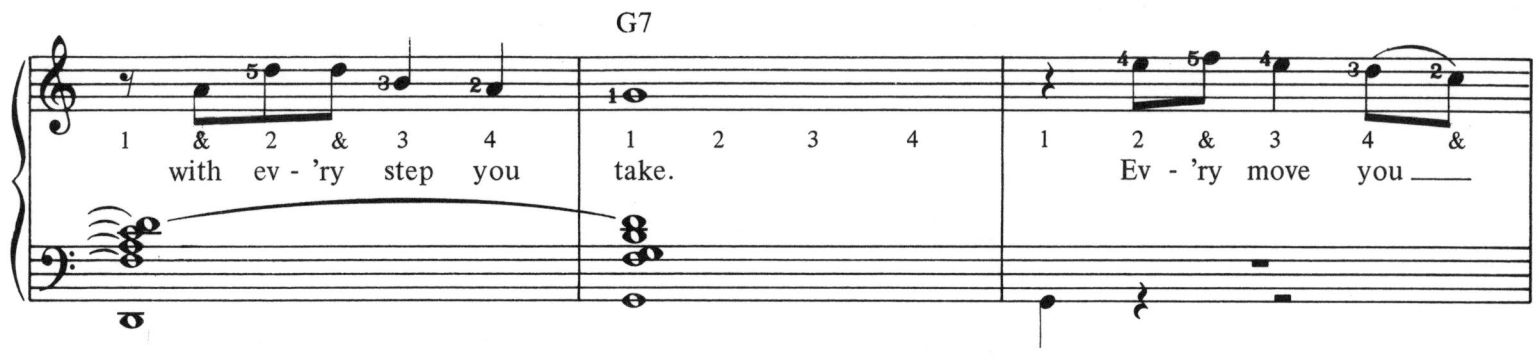
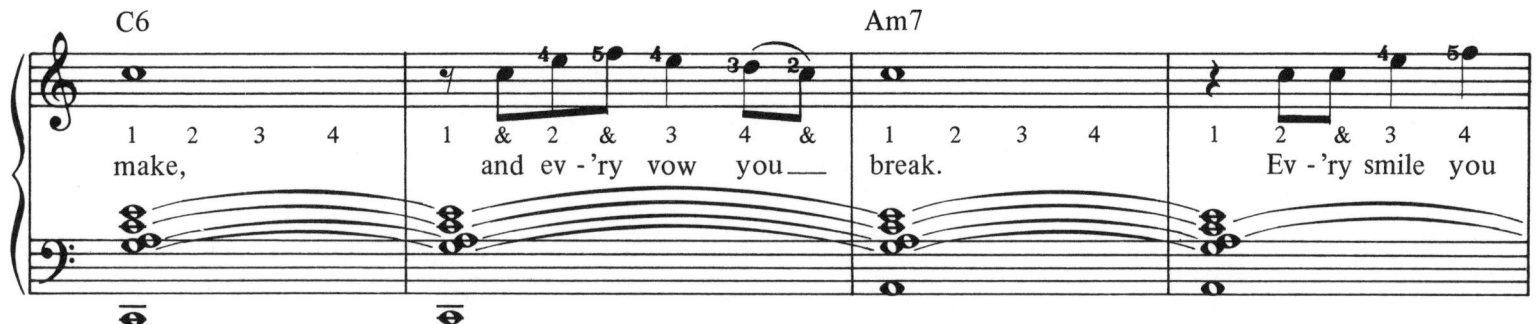
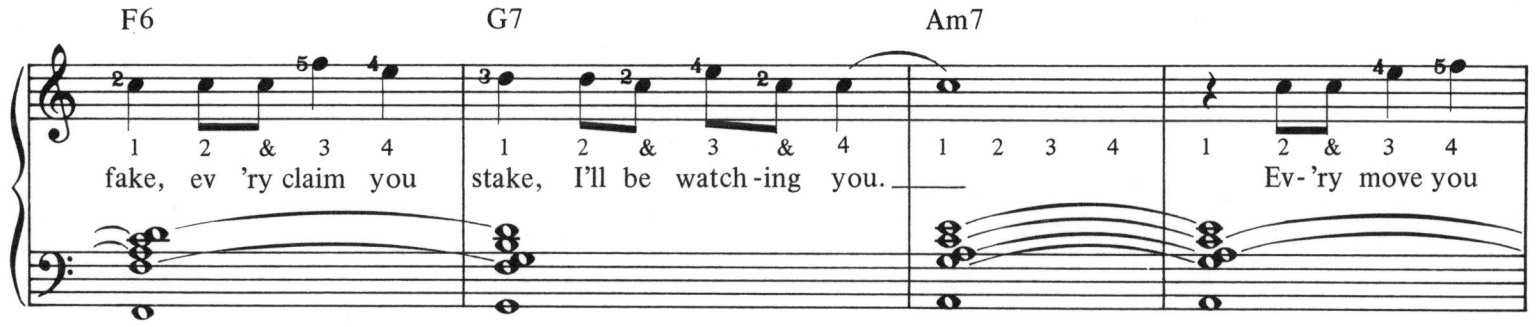
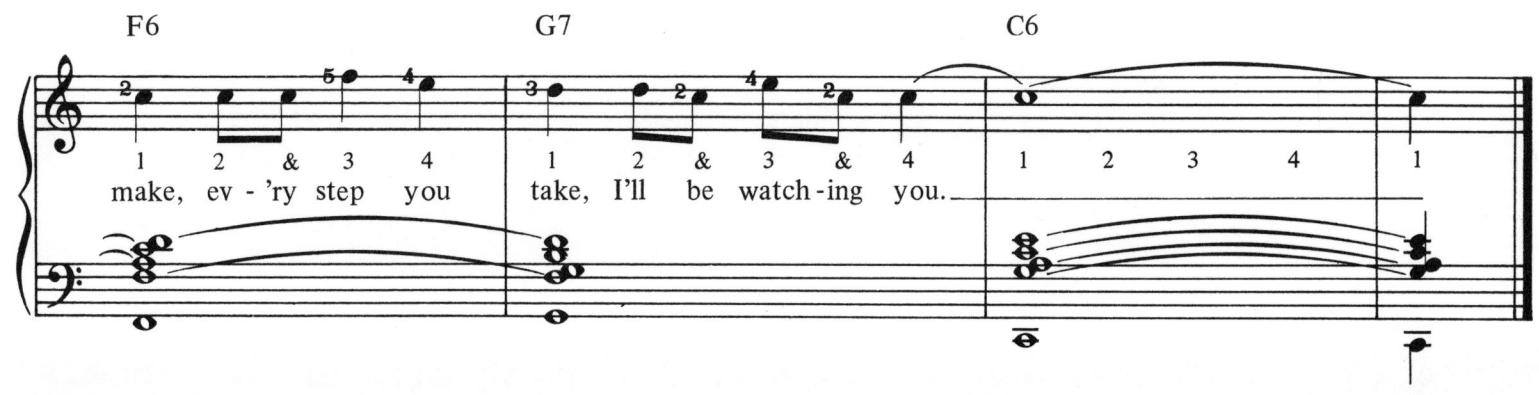

Dotted Crotchet (Dotted Quarter Note): ♩. or ♪·

A dot after a note increases its value by one half:

$$\text{𝅗𝅥} = \text{♩ ♩}$$

$$\text{𝅗𝅥.} = \text{♩ ♩ ♩}$$

The same rule applies to crotchets:

♩ (crotchet) = 1 beat

♩. (dotted crotchet) = 1½ beats

A Dotted Crotchet (1½ beats) is almost always accompanied by a single quaver (½ beat), making two full crotchet beats in all:

♩. ♪   1½ beats + ½ beat, total: 2 beats

or: ♪ ♪·   ½ beat + 1½ beats, total: 2 beats

The first of these two combinations: ♩. ♪ is the most common, and it appears frequently in the pieces which follow.

It is counted like this:

Silent Night (p. 35)

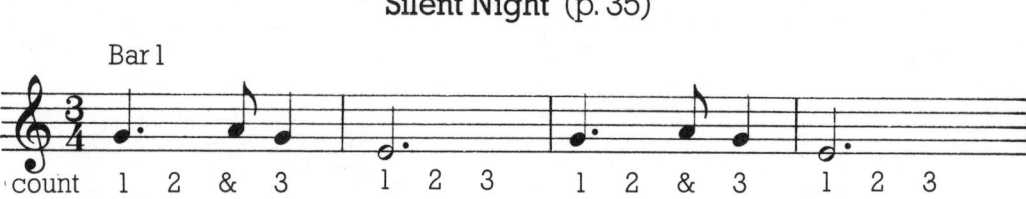

count 1 2 & 3   1 2 3   1 2 & 3   1 2 3

Bar 1. Play G on count 1.
Let this G continue into count 2.
Play A on the 'and' between counts 2 and 3.
Play G on count 3.

Silent Night
Traditional

Upper: vibraphone (with sustain) + string ensemble
Lower: flutes (with tremolo)
Pedal: 16' + 8'
Drums: waltz ♩ = 80

© Copyright 1977 by Dorsey Bros. Music Ltd., 8/9 Frith Street, London W1V 5TZ.
All Rights Reserved. International Copyright Secured.

New Melody Notes: Low G, A, B

Written:

My Own True Love (Tara's Theme)
Words by Mack David. Music by Max Steiner

Upper: clarinet (with, or without vibrato)
Lower: **flutes** (with tremolo) + strings (with sustain)
Pedal: 16' + 8'
Drums: bossa nova ♩ = 88

* 'Ledger Lines', see Dictionary Of Musical Terms (p. 45)

© Copyright 1941 by Remick Music Corp., New York.
© Copyright 1954 by Remick Music Corp., New York.
Warner Bros. Music Ltd., 17 Berners Street, London W1.
All Rights Reserved. International Copyright Secured.

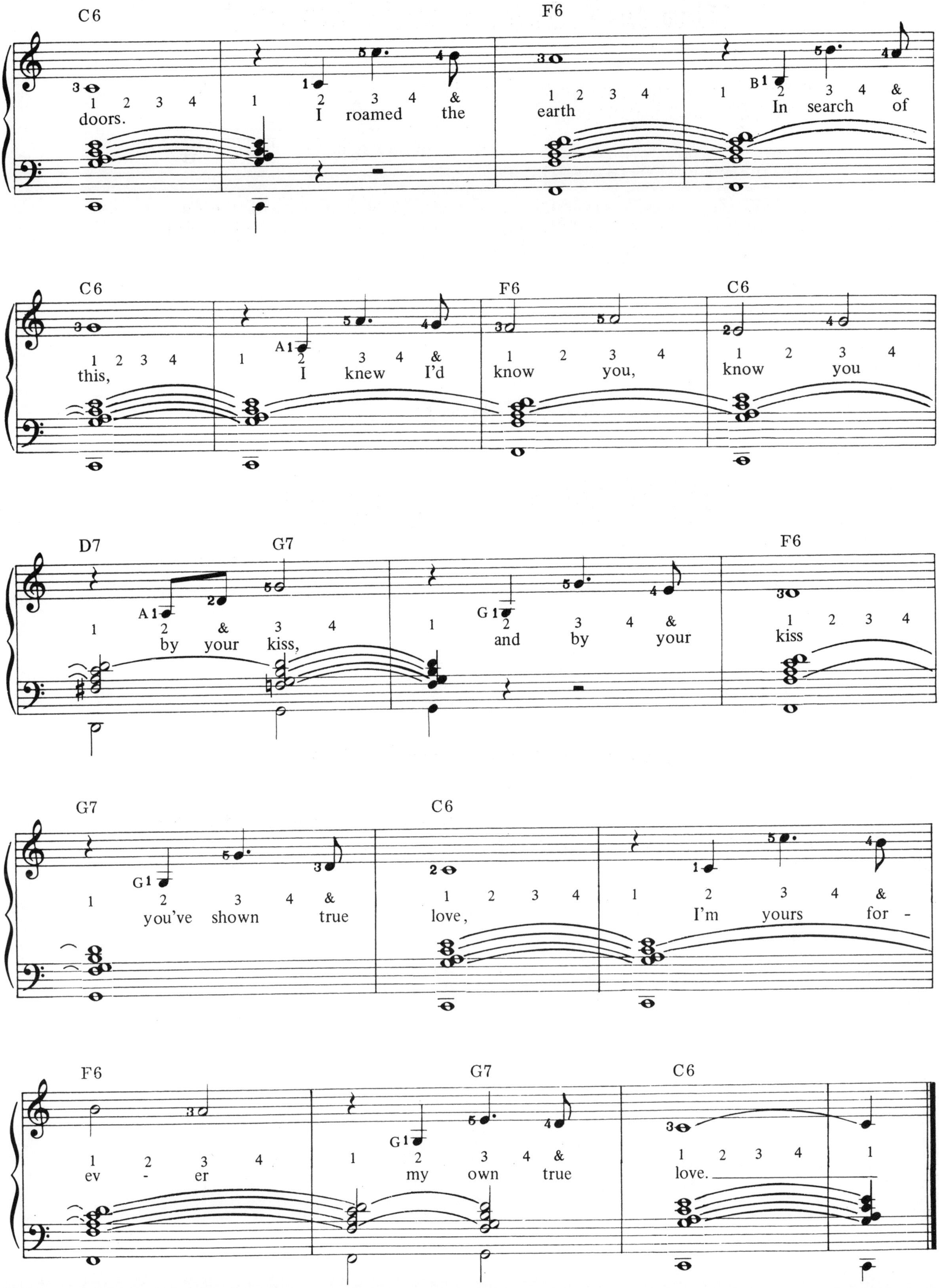
C6 F6
1 2 3 4 1 2 3 4 & 1 2 3 4 1 2 3 4 &
doors. I roamed the earth In search of
C6 F6 C6
1 2 3 4 1 2 3 4 & 1 2 3 4 1 2 3 4
this, I knew I'd know you, know you
D7 G7 F6
1 2 & 3 4 1 2 3 4 & 1 2 3 4
by your kiss, and by your kiss
G7 C6
1 2 3 4 & 1 2 3 4 1 2 3 4 &
you've shown true love, I'm yours for -
F6 G7 C6
1 2 3 4 1 2 3 4 & 1 2 3 4 1
ev - er my own true love.

Sharps ♯, Flats ♭, and Naturals ♮

- **♯** (SHARP) against a note means:- Play the nearest available note TO THE RIGHT of that note (usually a black note).

- **♭** (FLAT) against a note means:- Play the nearest available note TO THE LEFT of that note (usually a black note).

- **♮** (NATURAL) against a note means:- Cancel the SHARP or FLAT that was previously there. HOWEVER, when a new bar comes along THE SHARP OR FLAT IS AUTOMATICALLY CANCELLED.

New Chord: C7

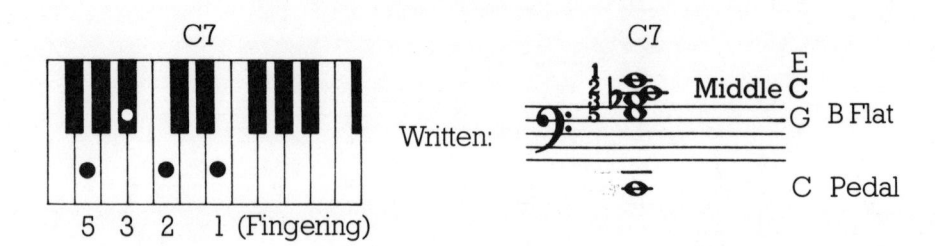

C7 — Fingering: 5 3 2 1

Written: E Middle C, G, B Flat, C Pedal

Two Pedal Notes Per Bar

In the next few pieces you point the rhythm further by playing a pedal note on every 3rd beat as well as on every 1st beat.

Release Me

Words & Music by Eddie Miller, Dub Williams, Robert Yount & Robert Harris

Upper: jazz guitar + string ensemble (with sustain)
Lower: **flutes** (with tremolo)
Pedal: bass guitar 8′
Drums: swing ♩ = 84

* "COMMON" Time. Another way of writing:- 4/4

© Copyright 1954 by Four Star Sales Co., U.S.A.
Palace Music Co. Ltd., London SE1 for the World (ex. North, Central & South America and Australasia).
All Rights Reserved. International Copyright Secured.

Top Of The World
Words by John Bettis. Music by Richard Carpenter.

Upper: flute (with vibrato)
Lower: strings (with sustain)
Pedal: 8'
Drums: swing ♩ = 80

Lyrics:
Such a feel-in's com-in' ov-er me.
Ev-'ry-thing I want the world to be
There is won-der in most ev-'ry-thing I see.
Not a cloud in the sky, got the sun in my eyes, and I won't be sur-prised if it's a

is now com-ing true, e-spe-cial-ly for me.
And the rea-son is clear, it's be-cause you are here, you're the near-est thing to hea-ven that I've

(2nd time only) F6

* 'CUT COMMON' TIME, see Dictionary Of Musical Terms (p. 45)

© Copyright 1972 by Almo Music Corp/Hammer and Nails Music, USA
All rights for the British Commonwealth of Nations (excluding Canada and Australasia) and the Republic of Eire controlled by
Rondor Music (London) Ltd, 10 Parsons Green, London SW6.
All Rights Reserved. International Copyright Secured.

1.
2.
G7
dream.
G7
seen.
I'm on the
C6
top of the world look - in'
F6
jump
down on cre - a - tion, and the
cross 2nd finger over thumb
C6
on - ly ex - pla - na - tion I can
G7
C6
find,
C7
is the
F6
love that I've
G7
found, ev - er
C6
since you've been a - round,
F6
your love's
cross 3rd finger over thumb
C6
put me at the
G7
top of the
C6
world.
stretch
F6
C6
extend hand

New Chord: Dm7

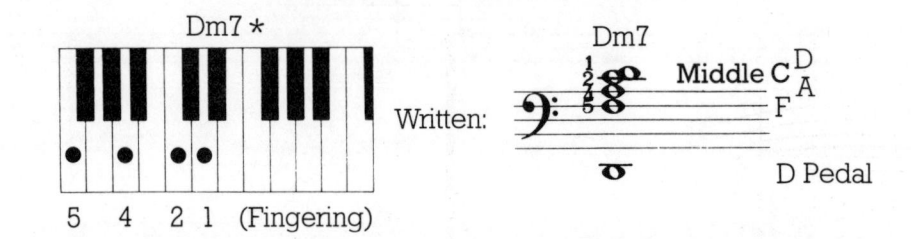

Goodnight Sweetheart
Words & Music by Ray Noble, Jimmy Campbell & Reg Connolly

Upper: string ensemble (with sustain)
Lower: **flutes** (with tremolo)
Pedal: 8′
Drums: swing ♩= 138

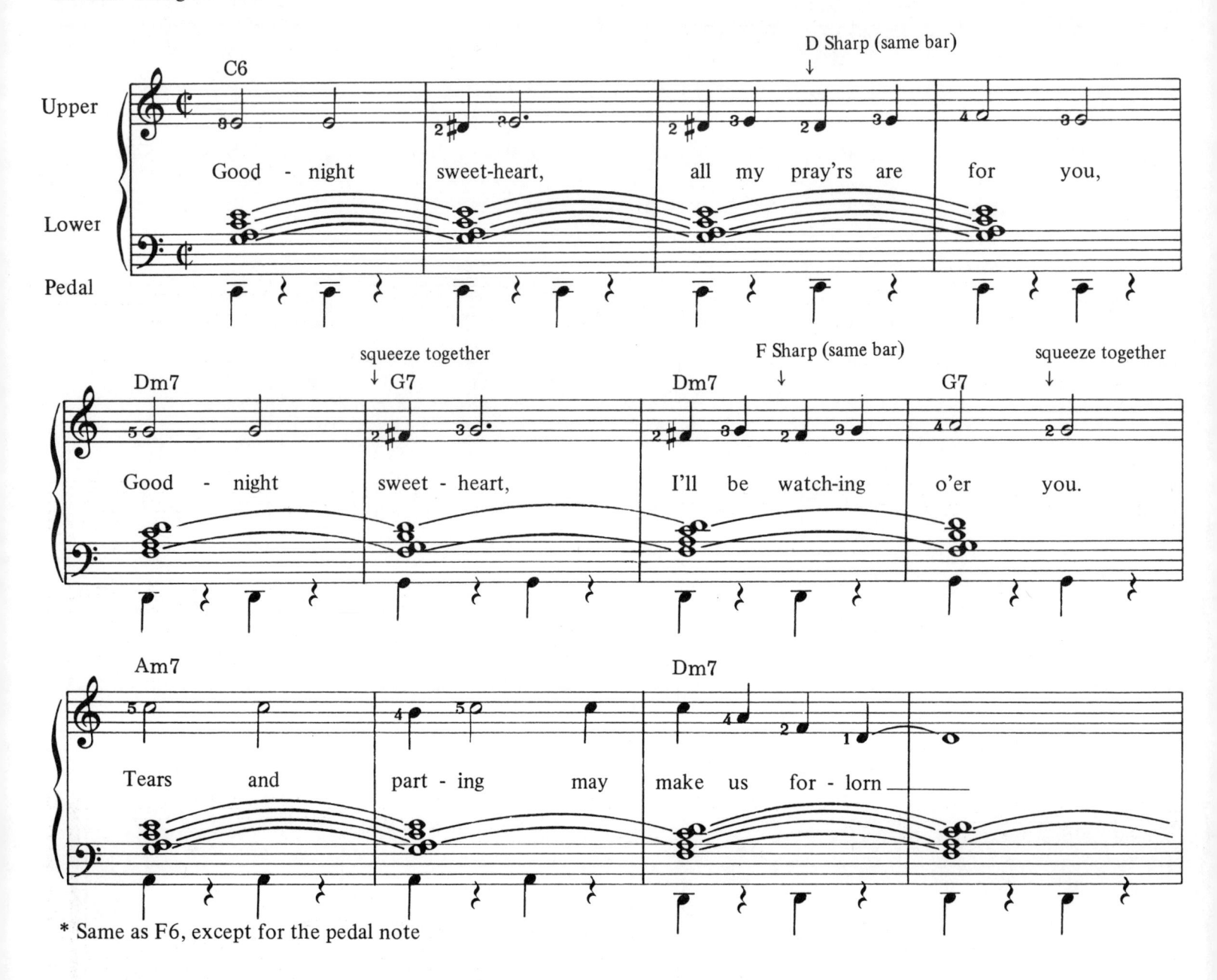

Good - night sweet-heart, all my pray'rs are for you,

Good - night sweet - heart, I'll be watch-ing o'er you.

Tears and part-ing may make us for-lorn

* Same as F6, except for the pedal note

© Copyright 1931 Campbell Connelly & Co. Ltd., 8/9 Frith Street, London W1V 5TZ.
All Rights Reserved. International Copyright Secured.

C6 Dm7 G7
but with the dawn a new day is born So I'll say
C6
change finger
Good - night sweet - heart, sleep will ban - ish sor - row,
Dm7 G7 Dm7 G7
squeeze together
Good - night sweet - heart, till we meet to - mor - row.
Am7 D7
Dreams en - fold you, in them dear I'll hold you,
cross 3rd finger over thumb
Dm7 G7
pass thumb underneath 2nd finger
C6
Good - night sweet - heart, good - night.

Reference Section
The Notes of both Keyboards (Manuals) and Pedal-Board

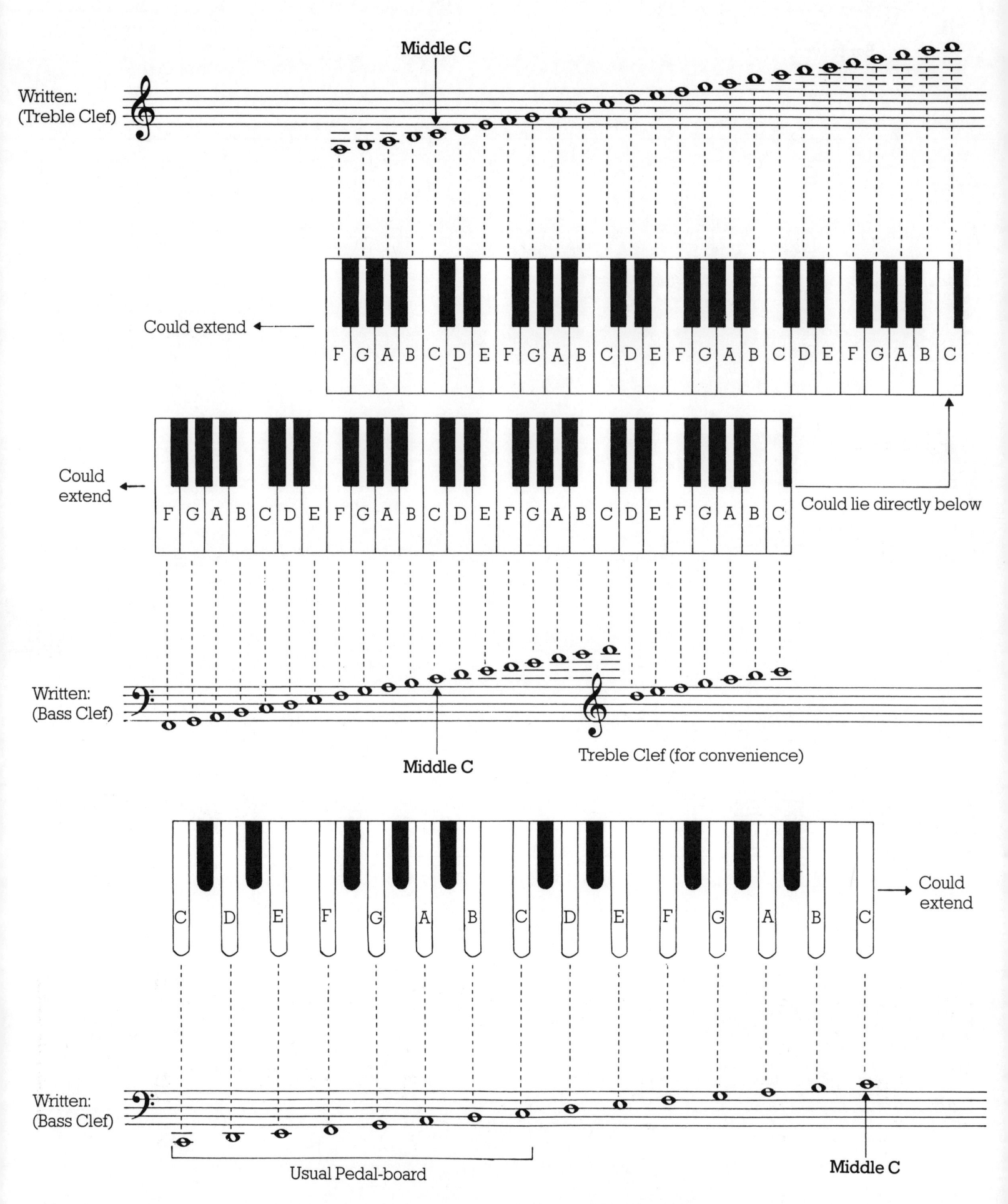

44

Dictionary of Musical Terms

Bar (Measure)	The result of the grouping of notes together for rhythmic purposes. The most common groupings are THREE notes to the BAR and FOUR notes to the BAR.
Bar Lines	The vertical lines which divide the music up into BARS.
Bass Clef 𝄢	The sign indicating the lower set (STAVE) of 5 lines upon which musical notes are written. On the organ the Bass Clef usually applies to the Lower Keyboard and Pedal-board only.
Beat	The rhythmic pulse behind most music.
Chord	Three or more notes played together.
Common Time 𝄴	Four Crotchets (Quarter Notes) per bar. Another way of writing: $\frac{4}{4}$
Crotchet (Quarter Note) ♩	A measure of the duration of a musical note. The Crotchet is usually used as the basic 'beat' or pulse of the music.
Crotchet (Quarter) Rest 𝄽	A silence lasting for a Crotchet (or 1 beat).
Cut Common Time 𝄵	$\frac{2}{2}$; a feeling of TWO MINIMS in a bar, rather than FOUR CROTCHETS. Usually occurs in faster pieces where it is more convenient to count 2 than 4.
Dotted Crotchet (Dotted Quarter Note) ♩.	A Crotchet and a half; three Quavers; 1½ Crotchet beats.
Dotted Crotchet (Dotted Quarter) Rest 𝄽.	A silence lasting for a Dotted Crotchet (1½ beats).
Dotted Minim (Dotted Half Note) ♩.	A note lasting for 3 Crotchet beats.
Dotted Minim (Dotted Half) Rest ▬.	A silence lasting for 3 Crotchet beats.
Drum Rhythm	The drum accompaniment which can be obtained from most organs.
Flat ♭	The sign which lowers a note (i.e. moves it to the LEFT) by the nearest possible distance on the keyboard.
Ledger Line	The basic staves of five lines upon which music is written are not sufficient to cover every note played. Therefore small 'Ledger Lines' have to be used, each indicating the real full length line which would lie in that place. 'Middle C' is an example of a note on a LEDGER LINE. 'Bottom C' on the pedal-board is an example of a note requiring two LEDGER LINES.

Manual	Keyboard.
Melody	The Tune, or Air.
Metronome	An instrument capable of indicating the speed of a piece of music. The conventional metronome consists of a pendulum device (adjustable).
Middle C	The most central 'C' note on a piano keyboard. On the organ it will probably not be central, owing to the fact that there are two separate keyboards, usually overlapping each other, and each one having its own 'Middle C.' Note also that on the organ the position of 'Middle C' can alter (i.e. become higher or lower) with the changing of the Stops. See the Keyboard Chart p. 44, for the most probable position of the 'Middle C's.' (The Lower Keyboard 'Middle C' as shown is almost sure to be right, regardless of Stops).
Minim (Half Note) ♩	A note lasting for 2 Crotchet beats.
Minim (Half) Rest ▬	A silence lasting for a Minim (2 Crotchet beats).
Natural ♮	The sign which cancels a SHARP or a FLAT.
N.C.	No Chord.
Quaver (Eighth Note) ♪ ♫	Half a Crotchet beat. In other words, there will be two Quavers to every Crotchet beat.
Quaver (Eighth) Rest ʼ	A silence lasting for half a Crotchet beat.
Repeat Signs	A series of devices used to save space, and the unnecessary turning of pages. They are as follows:-

‖: :‖

The section between the two signs is to be repeated. If there is no earlier Repeat Mark, go back to the beginning of the piece.

|1   :‖

The bar, or bars, enclosed by the bracket will be played on the 1st time through only. (The player will then go back in order to make the repeat).

|2   :‖

The bar, or bars, enclosed by the bracket will be played on the 2nd time through only. The player will then play on (unless he has already reached the end of the piece).

Semibreve (Whole Note) 𝐨   A note lasting for four Crotchet beats.

Semibreve (Whole) Rest ▬   A silence lasting for a Semibreve (or 4 Crotchet beats). Also used for a bar's rest, regardless of Time Signature.

Sharp ♯   The sign which raises a note (i.e. moves it to the RIGHT) by the nearest possible distance on the keyboard.

Stave   The 5 horizontal lines upon which music is written.

Tie   A device used to make a note last longer. Only applies when the notes connected by the curved line are the same. (When a curved line joins different notes it could mean: 1. play the notes smoothly, 2. a word in the lyric is to be sung right through the notes concerned).

Time Signature   Appears at the beginning of a piece to denote how many beats per bar, and whether the beats consist of Crotchets (the usual), or some other time notes.

 NOTE: If there were two minims (half notes) per bar, the Time Signature would read $\frac{2}{2}$; if there were six quavers (eighth notes) per bar, the Time Signature would read $\frac{6}{8}$; and so on.

Treble Clef   The sign indicating the upper set (STAVE) of 5 lines upon which musical notes are written. On the organ the Treble Clef usually applies to the Upper Keyboard, but occasionally – when playing very high on the Lower Keyboard for example – it is more convenient to use the Treble Clef for that keyboard also. (See Keyboard Chart, p. 44).

Chord Chart

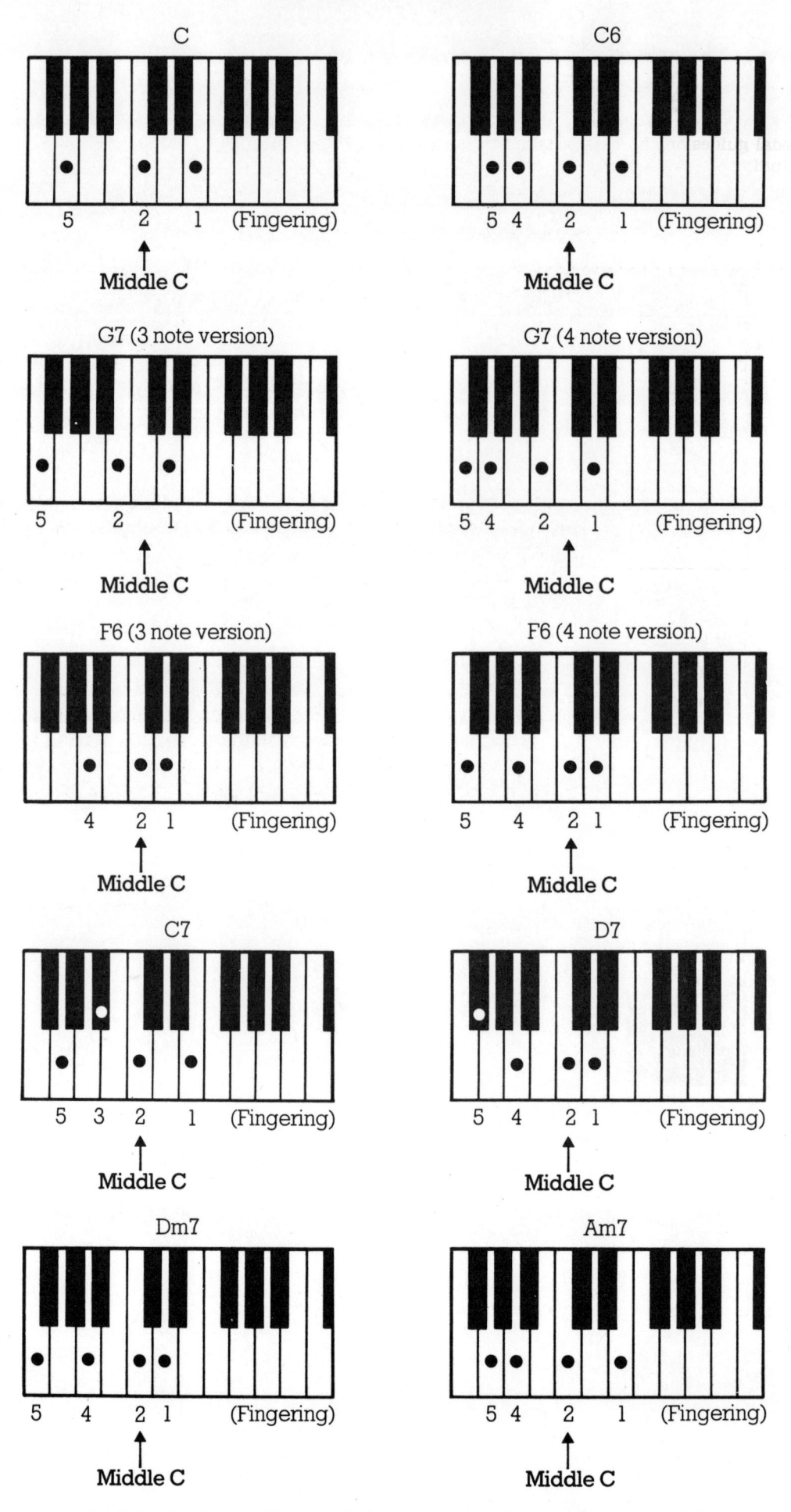

C — Fingering: 5 2 1 (Middle C is the note played by finger 2)

C6 — Fingering: 5 4 2 1 (Middle C is the note played by finger 2)

G7 (3 note version) — Fingering: 5 2 1 (Middle C is the note played by finger 1)

G7 (4 note version) — Fingering: 5 4 2 1 (Middle C is the note played by finger 1)

F6 (3 note version) — Fingering: 4 2 1 (Middle C is the note played by finger 2)

F6 (4 note version) — Fingering: 5 4 2 1 (Middle C is the note played by finger 2)

C7 — Fingering: 5 3 2 1 (Middle C is the note played by finger 2)

D7 — Fingering: 5 4 2 1 (Middle C is the note played by finger 2)

Dm7 — Fingering: 5 4 2 1 (Middle C is the note played by finger 2)

Am7 — Fingering: 5 4 2 1 (Middle C is the note played by finger 2)

(Pedals play Letter Names of chords, e.g. with Dm7 play Pedal 'D')